# Napa Navigator

Ralph & Lahni de Amicis

Cuore Libre Publishing
Napa California

Published by
Cuore Libre Publishing, The Amicis Winery Guides
Napa, California

To Order Copies Phone 707-235-2648
Email: Lahni@AmicisTours.com or go to
www.AmicisTours.com/napanavigator.html

Printed in the United States of America

Disclaimer: We create these books through extensive research but make no guarantees for the accuracy of the information included herein, and accept no responsibility for any losses or inconvenience you may suffer from using this product.  Important:  These tours are designed to be as safe and enjoyable as possible but alcohol and driving are a risky mix. It should be approached cautiously by having a designated or professional driver. Have a fun day in Wine Country and come back again and again.

Ralph & Lahni de Amicis

# Contents

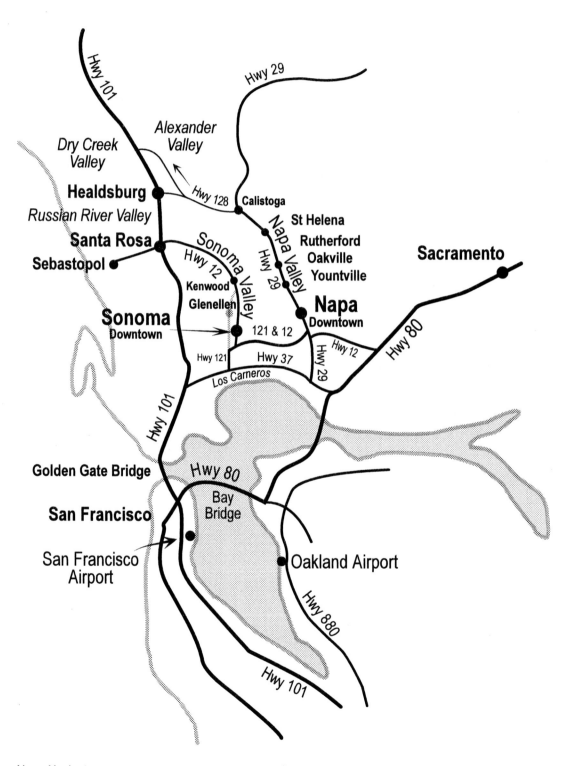

# Introduction to the Napa Navigator

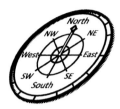

Wine touring is a fun way to spend the day, but Wine Country is Farm Country, so many destinations are spread out along narrow, winding roads. If you want to make the best use of your time, the more you know and the clearer your maps, the better your day is going to be. We are tour guides, so our books contain the information we need to create smooth and enjoyable experiences for our guests. As we develop each new book we work hard at making the information clearer and more accessible. Coincidentally, it is the same information you probably need to safely and efficiently navigate the roads and tastings rooms. To best enjoy touring in wine country you need four things: First, navigation tips. Second, basic tasting room etiquette and ways to get the most out of the winery experience. Third, honest descriptions of the 250 plus wineries that you can visit, either by just walking in, or making an easy appointment. And Fourth, easy to read maps. We just described the Napa Navigator! Here is a bonus, to make our books easier to read in a car the text and maps are printed with large, clear fonts.

The navigation and tasting room tips come first in short, concise chapters. Next is the winery directory. Because we don't accept advertising and base our reviews on our client's experience, they are realistic pictures of what you can expect. Finally, there are the maps, which are done in black on white making them easy to read and to write notes on. We suggest a red marker! Rather than cramming every winery onto one map, we divide them based upon popular areas, because people tend to spend much of their day within two or three connected AVA's (American Vitacultural Areas). Each winery's listing denotes the **MAP** where they can be found.

The *Map Directory* on page 79 divides them into four groups. The first are regional maps in the 'How to Get to Napa' chapter. The second group, which starts after the Winery Directory, includes various themed tours, accompanied by brief descriptions and driving instructions. These are well tested (and very safe) itineraries that work by themselves, or as a base to improvise upon. The next map group consists of Area Overviews including descriptions of prominent wineries. Finally, there are maps of various areas that show more of the wineries than either the Tour or Overview Maps. In that way each map is less cluttered and easier to read while you drive from winery to winery. So enjoy and come back soon!

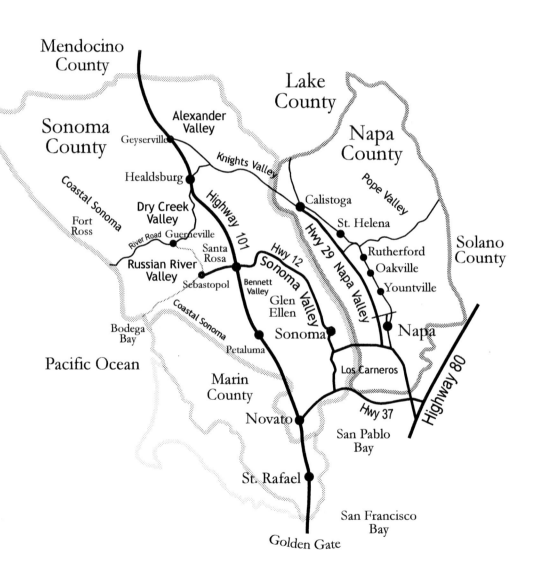

# Chapter 1: Traveling to Wine Country

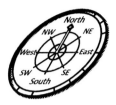

To reach both the Napa Valley and Sonoma from San Francisco, our favorite route is to cross over the Golden Gate on Highway 101. To Napa the Bay Bridge route is a little shorter, but between traffic on the bridge and Hwy 80 the time is the same, and the Golden Gate Route is prettier. In 25 to 20 minutes you will exit at Highway 37 East, heading through Sonoma County. Turn left at Highway 121 (There is a traffic light and signs to Sonoma and Napa). After the light you will pass some Sonoma Carneros wineries: Ram's Gate, Viansa, Jacuzzi, Cline and Gloria Ferrer. At the next (blinking) traffic light, turn right following the signs towards Napa.

**To the Sonoma Plaza**: Take the next left, (A Light) Highway 12 North. There will be signs indicating Sonoma. That road is also called Broadway and it will take you directly to the historic Sonoma Plaza. This is one of the most historic spots in California and a charming place to stop for shopping and a meal. **To get the Sonoma Valley** continue on Highway 12, which turns left at the Plaza. In five miles you will be at the first vineyards. This beautiful region is also known as the Valley of the Moon. At the northern end of the Valley is the city of Santa Rosa, and beyond that is the Russian River Valley. To reach Northern Sonoma from San Francisco a better route is recommended below.

**To Get to Napa.** When Highway 121 bears right at the flashing signal after Gloria Ferrer continue straight on Highway 121 for about fifteen minutes. to the T intersection with Highway 29. Navigation Tip: When you see very French looking Domaine Carneros (A good first stop for sparkling wines) towering to the right you are in the Los Carneros section of Napa. Five minutes after that you will be at the T intersection with Highway 29 where you should turn left to go north to the Napa Valley.

The Valley is about 30 miles long and 1 to 5 miles wide. Driving up Highway 29 will bring you to Yountville (Home of Domaine Chandon), then Oakville, and Rutherford, the heart of the Valley.

Look for the Oakville Grocery (7856 St Helena Hwy Highway 29, Oakville CA). This area includes a profusion of world class wineries: Robert Mondavi, Opus One, Nickel and Nickel, Sequoia Grove, Turnbull, Cakebread, Sawyer, St. Supery, Rubicon, B.V. and Peju. Farther north is St Helena and at the top of the Valley, Calistoga. There are hundreds of wineries to visit throughout the valley.

**To Northern Sonoma**: Coming from San Francisco the best way to reach Northern Sonoma including Santa Rosa, Healdsburg, the Russian River Valley, the Dry Creek Valley and Alexander Valley is to continue north on Highway 101 past Santa Rosa to their exits, River Road, Downtown Healdsburg and Dry Creek Road. In light traffic the Northern Sonoma wine regions are about one and a half to two hours driving time from San Francisco.

**Timing Hints**: Start early! This is farm country where everything important happens during the day. Wineries are generally open 10 to 5 (In Northern Sonoma 11-4 except in Healdsburg). Allow 30 to 45 minutes for visiting each winery. Most winery tours require an hour.

Allow fifteen minutes traveling between wineries. Add one hour for lunch after the second winery to maintain stable blood sugar levels and promote tasting endurance. Visiting three wineries requires four to five hours, not including travel time to and from wine country. Note: Check the listing to see if picnicking is permitted. Only a winery's own wine can be consumed on their property, and the nicer ones will loan you glasses for your picnic.

Visiting more than three wineries requires a disciplined designated driver, or hiring a car and driver, which is cheaper, safer and more fun than a D.U.I. Splitting this cost with friends or family makes it reasonable, especially in comparison to legal fees, bail money and stress.

To visit five wineries or more we suggest having a professional driver since few designated drivers want to put up with that much chaos in their car.

**Dress Code:** "Wine Country Casual" is the standard. In other words, you can't look too good, but you could look too formal. It is normally 10 to 15 degrees warmer here than in San Francisco, although suddenly cool after sundown, so bring a light jacket or sweater for evening's out and cave visits. Remember that wineries are farms and ranches, so unless you are limiting yourself to only the most commercial places, wear comfortable shoes suitable for the country.

# Chapter 2: Wine Country Navigation

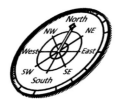

Napa's main road, Hwy 29, (St. Helena Hwy) bisects America's most valuable vineyards and the towns of Napa, Yountville, Rutherford, Oakville, St. Helena and Calistoga. It is 4 lanes south of Yountville and 2 lanes north with turning lanes at intersections and wineries. To the east of Hwy 29 near the Vaca Mountains is the Silverado Trail which starts in the city of Napa and travels the length of the valley. It's a scenic alternative on busy traffic days.

There are numerous crossroads that connect Hwy 29 and the Silverado Trail like rungs on a ladder. To reach the base of the Trail take the Trancas Street exit off Hwy 29, , bear to the right, and in about ten minutes turn left at the traffic light for the Silverado Trail. There are wineries on both north/south roads and the Hwy 29 wineries in Oakville and Rutherford are packed together pretty tightly. On saturdays north bound traffic often backs up going through St. Helena. To avoid that turn right on Zinfandel Lane and take that to the Silverado Trail.

To reach St Helena from the Silverado Trail take Pope Street to the south edge of town (the bridge is narrow and curving). Or, Pratt Street brings you to Hwy 29 just north of town and south of Beringer. A little further on you can take Deer Park which is a popular crossroad. Returning south at the end of the day via the Silverado Trail is a good way to avoid the back ups in St. Helena, Rutherford, Oakville and the City of Napa.

**Recognizing Street and Winery Signs:** In Napa Valley road signs are placed a couple hundred feet before the intersection. At the intersection, markings are painted on the asphalt. By late summer bushes obscure the roads and the paint wears off so take your time. The cross roads are narrow and the bridges are mostly a hundred years old so take it easy.

Winery signs appear various distances before the entrance, if at all. They use small, white on blue signs about 30 inches wide by 10 inches high. The best strategy is to know the winery's address and watch for the numbers. Some small wineries only use street numbers.

# Chapter 3: What to Expect in a Tasting Room

A tasting normally includes 1 to 2 ounces each of 4 to 5 wines in a sequence from a light white like Chardonnay or Sauvignon Blanc to a heavy red like Merlot or Cabernet Sauvignon. There is normally a fee based on the cost of the wine. You can share tastings and there are buckets to pour the excess wine out. The idea is to taste, not get drunk. The sense of smell is critical so don't wear heavy perfumes or colognes and avoid lipstick which leaves oils on the crystal glasses.

Start by swirling the wine to open the flavors. Do this by setting the glass on the tasting bar, holding it by the base and making little, energetic circles. Then, holding the glass by the stem, tilt it and inhale the bouquet. Tilting the glass to about 45 degrees and placing your nose inside the lower edge of the glass allows you to smell the fruit instead of the rising alcohol, which has its own scent. When a wine has been aged for an extended period of time in oak barrels, which is common with the Bordeaux reds, you'll notice the difference in the scent when you swirl it to the left or the right. Swirling counterclockwise reveals more of barrel flavors, while swirling clockwise brings out the fruit.

Next, take a sip and hold the wine in your mouth, letting it reach all the parts of your tongue and its diverse taste buds to clear your palate of previous flavors. Now, swirl and sip again. With this sip you truly taste the wine. Enjoy! If you don't like the wine, or you've had enough, dump the excess. There is plenty more to come so protect your tasting endurance.

**Hints**: Don't wear white. Read the winery tasting notes while you sample to help identify the flavors. The flavors they mention occur naturally in the grapes, they are not added. Inhale the bouquet gently because the sensors are at the front of the nose. The nose recognizes over 2400 different scents while the palette identifies 5 major flavors, so the mouth feel is critically important; is it silky, syrupy or sharp? Professional tasters spit the wine out which is more critically accurate, but less fun. By the way, tipping the pourer is not common, nor expected. The best way to say thank you for a great tasting experience is to buy their wine. It is, after all, the world's best souvenir, after jewelry.

# Chapter 4: Improving Your Tasting Endurance

Successful and enjoyable wine tasting is all about pacing yourself and extending your tasting endurance. You do that by starting with a good breakfast with plenty of fats and protein, no pancakes and syrup. Then eat again after every two wineries, once again including fats and protein. This will keep your blood sugar levels steady and prevent tiredness. Avoid soft and sweet cheeses since the milk sugar will contribute to the problem. Better foods to snack on are nuts, meats, fish, and hard cheeses, and of course, Italian or French bread to soak up some wine.

The other important secret is to drink audacious amounts of water in between tastings. Two or four ounces of water to each ounce of wine, so a bottle of water after each tasting. That way the alcohol is diffused throughout your bloodstream, so instead of feeling drunk your head will feel illuminated and even your feet will feel good. That large infusion of water will also help overcome the other main complaint, red wine headaches.

## Sulfites or Dehydration

Often sulfites are blamed for red wine headaches, but most of the time they are not the culprit, especially with premium wines where very few added sulfites are used in the process. High sulfite levels are more often a culprit with cheaper wines where their purifying qualities overcome some of the problems of lower quality, machine harvested grapes. Dehydration of the brain is usually the problem and it comes from three sources, alcohols, phenols and hot weather.

## The Wine Country Environment

During the main growing season, May to November, there is very little rain and daytime humidity can stay around twenty-five percent. The twenty to twenty eight inches of rain comes from December to April when the hills turn so green and misty that you would think that you were in Ireland. Alcohol is dehydrating and California wines are typically 'hotter' (higher in alcohol) than European wines with 14 to 16% being common. Between 7% and 14% is a table wine, with the common European wines being about 9-12%. Most people are chronically dehydrated so it doesn't take much to push them over the edge.

## Young Tannins

Tannins give red wines the ability to improve with age and are found in the skins and seeds. Since red wines sit on the skins to extract color and flavor they're higher in tannins than whites, and thick-skinned grapes like Cabernet Sauvignon are richest in them. One of the grape components, phenols, are created when the vines are stressed. Old, knurly vines produce more phenols than new vines. The phenols are an important part of creating character and depth of flavor. Tannins and phenols are both very dehydrating. Over time, they soften and become more palatable and, depending upon the wines, that could take three, five or ten years.

It would be nice if the wineries would pour the wine when it was really ready to drink, with soft, rounded tannins. Instead, they pour them as young as they can get away with. Why? Because they want you to buy them now, not three to five years from now when they are ready! As a result these wines are very dehydrating and they'll give you headaches unless you drink plenty of water. Bring four 12 ounce bottles per person and an ice chest to keep them cold. Then drink them in the course of the day. When it's hot out, which it often is up in the valleys, it's easy to drink a lot of water. Having the ice chest handy is great when you buy bottles of wine on a hot day, because the ice chest is a great place to protect your purchases from the heat.

# Chapter 5: Increasing Your Tasting Sensitivity

It is surprising that people who should know better still make rookie mistakes when planning wine tours. That may seem a little harsh, but for all of the beautiful scenery and great buildings, the relationship between the human palate and the flavor of the wine is an essential part of the equation, and yet people don't plan their tours around that.

If you got up in the morning and someone who loves you set a cup of coffee in front of you, and in response you said, "No darling, this morning I'm starting with Cabernet Sauvignon." That would raise some eyebrows. With all of those tannins, a Cab Sauv is a little hard on the taste buds right out of bed. The great thing about a big red is that it can reach through all of the other flavors you encounter during the day and still get the palate's attention.

There are three main levels of tasters; tolerant, sensitive and hyper-sensitive. The difference is the quantity of taste buds on your palate. Many men are tolerant, so they can drink their coffee black, or with some cream, or however they can get it. Many women are sensitive tasters exhibiting more refinement, and a smaller number of people are hyper-sensitive tasters. They're the ones that say 'yeeech, that's horrible', while the tolerant taster is taking a second sip.

Because men tend to be tolerant tasters the tannic reds with lots of punch appeal to them, less so to women who prefer the complexity of Pinot Noir. But, during a day of tasting, palates can become clogged and insensitive, especially if they *drink* the wine. Professionals spit out the wine to maintain their sobriety and to protect their livers.

But, the most germane reason they spit is because alcohol numbs their perception. After a few sips everything tastes good, and then it all tastes the same. The only way to taste two or three dozen wines and still do a clear analysis is to spit them out but no one on vacation wants to do that.

When you plan a day of tasting wine, start with light-weight wines that require a fresh palate to appreciate; Chardonnay, Sauvignon Blanc, Riesling, Pinot Noir or Sparkling Wine (normally made from chard and pinot). After that, move on to tasting the Syrah and Zinfandel, and then finish the day with the Cabernet Sauvignon. Don't visit a Pinot house at the end of the day when your palate is coated and anesthetized because you won't appreciate it.

What you don't want to do is start the day at Opus One, or the To Kalon room at Robert Mondavi where they specialize in tannic, long aging reds. Instead, start the day at Domaine Carneros, Domaine Chandon, Artesa, Goosecross or Trefethen, places that offer some variety and lightness of flavor. That's one of the keys to a great day of wine tasting.

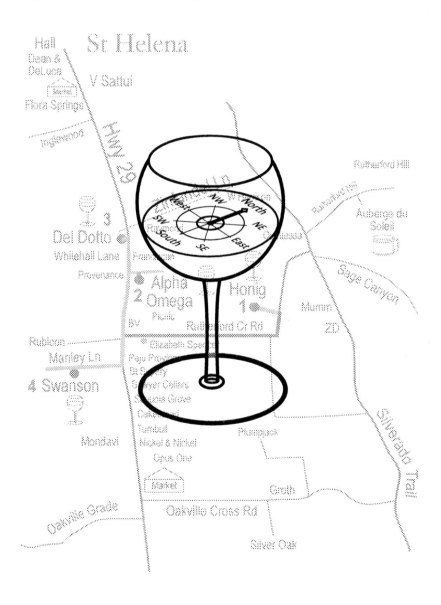

# Chapter 6: Directory of Tours, Overviews and Maps

## Maps

# Overview: Touring the Napa Valley Wineries

Even though you will recognize many winery names from the labels on your store shelves at home, consider visiting wineries that you have never heard of before. Many wonderful wineries in Napa sell all of their wine through their tasting room and wine club. You are not going to find bad wine in Napa, the community standards are too high. Be brave and explore!

Of course, there is no way to talk about Wine Country without talking about Napa. We looked at Sonoma first because it is closer to the Golden Gate, but Napa is America's most famous wine region and that is reflected in the quantity of wineries, and the high prices they can command for their wines.

Napa county contains an amazing diversity of climates and soils, and most of the land that is suitable for vineyards is planted with vines, about 9% of the county. The rest of the land, other than wineries, homes, stores, hotels and restaurants, is covered with pastures and trees, mostly oak, redwoods, mountain laurel, eucalyptus and red-barked madrona. Trees influence the wine's flavors, and some famous Oakville vineyards owe their subtle spice to the large stands of fragrant eucalyptus nearby.

The valley is thirty miles long by five miles wide, so you can easily travel the length and breadth of it in a day. But, since many wineries are close together, depending on your tour, you could spend the entire day tasting within a five-mile radius.

If you are coming over the Golden Gate and through Sonoma county, follow Highway 121 to the T intersection with Highway 29. Turning left will bring you north to the Napa Valley. On the way you will pass the city of Napa, not obvious beyond the highway barriers. In a few miles and a few traffic lights you will be in the Valley.

South of Oakville there are few wineries directly on the side of the road. However, there are some very good ones that are accessible on the side roads: Trefethen, Andretti, Biale, Monticello, Laird, Elyse, Bell and Domaine Chandon. Just past the Oakville Grocery there are a profusion of world class wineries in a row: Opus One, Nickel and Nickel (appointment), Robert Mondavi, Sequoia Grove, Turnbull, Cakebread (appointment), St. Supery, Peju, Rubicon, Beaulieu (BV), Grgich Hills, Alpha Omega, Franciscan and Whitehall.

There is still more than half of the valley to the north, and to the right of Hwy 29 is the Silverado Trail, which has its own collection of wineries. We list about 250 Napa wineries that you can easily visit with or without an appointment, but there are about three times that many producing wines that are open mostly to industry insiders and collectors.

# The Napa Valley

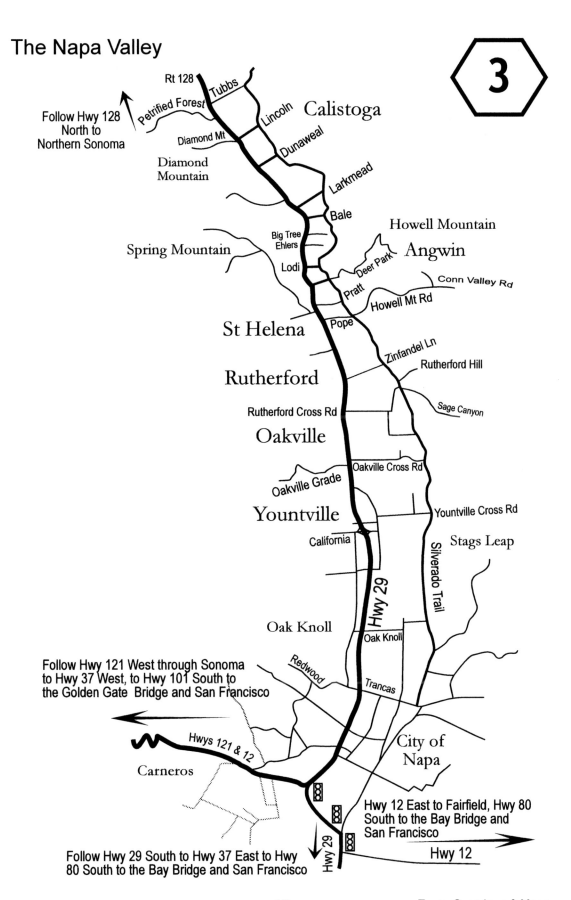

3

Follow Hwy 128 North to Northern Sonoma

Rt 128
Petrified Forest
Tubbs
Lincoln
Calistoga
Diamond Mt
Dunaweal
Diamond Mountain
Larkmead
Bale
Big Tree
Ehlers
Spring Mountain
Howell Mountain
Angwin
Deer Park
Lodi
Conn Valley Rd
Pratt
Howell Mt Rd
Pope
St Helena
Zinfandel Ln
Rutherford Hill
Rutherford
Sage Canyon
Rutherford Cross Rd
Oakville
Oakville Cross Rd
Oakville Grade
Yountville Cross Rd
Yountville
Stags Leap
California
Silverado Trail
Hwy 29
Oak Knoll
Oak Knoll
Follow Hwy 121 West through Sonoma to Hwy 37 West, to Hwy 101 South to the Golden Gate Bridge and San Francisco
Redwood
Trancas
Hwys 121 & 12
City of Napa
Carneros
Hwy 12 East to Fairfield, Hwy 80 South to the Bay Bridge and San Francisco
Follow Hwy 29 South to Hwy 37 East to Hwy 80 South to the Bay Bridge and San Francisco
Hwy 29
Hwy 12

Tours, Overviews & Maps

# Tour 1: Napa Favorites that are Always Fun

**Goosecross Cellars,** 1119 State Ln. Yountville. A small, charming winery with a diverse list of well-made wines. Walk past the winery equipment to the barrel room tasting. Hrs: 10 -4:30 by instant appt. Show up! TF: $ *They do wonderful seminars* by appointment. **Wines**: Viognier, Chenin Blanc, Sauv Blanc, Chard, Sparkling Rosé, Cab Sauv, Zin, Merlot, Pinot Noir, Syrah, Blends.
***Directions:*** *Follow Yountville Cr. Rd to Hwy 29 (requires a quick left and a right turn). At Hwy 29 turn right to Oakville Cr. Rd, turn right to Plumpjack Winery. The sign is before the hill on the left: 3.6 miles, approx 10 minutes.*

**Plumpjack Winery,** 620 Oakville Cross Rd. Oakville. This is a very friendly winery with well-known wines. Surprisingly small for such a good label. The staff is great and the gift shop is fun. The winery faces the tasting room. Hrs: 10–4   TF: $$ - $$$  **Wines**: Cab Sauv, Chard, Merlot, Syrah.
***Directions:*** *Backtrack to Oakville Grocery: 2.1 miles, 5 minutes. Pick up picnic items to eat at the Rutherford Hill Winery's picnic tables.*
***Directions:*** *From Oakville Grocery turn right to Rutherford Road, turn right, follow it to the Silverado Trail, turn left and then a quick right onto Rutherford Hill Rd. Look for the large boulder-sign at the intersection, follow it to the top of the hill to Rutherford Hill Winery: 5.3 miles, approx 10 minutes.*

**Rutherford Hill Winery,** 200 Rutherford Hill Rd. Rutherford. This is a great mid-sized winery owned by the Terlato family who also owns Chimney Rock. This is a great place to picnic under the olive trees with wonderful views. Good wines, great staff & gift shop and *one of the best tours.* Hrs: 10–5   TF: $$ 707.963.1871  **Wines**: Zin Port, Merlot, Cab Sauv, Sangiovese, Blends, Petite Verdot, Chard, Syrah, Malbec, Sauv Blanc.
***Directions:*** *At  Silverado Trail turn left. Mumm is on the right, 1.6 miles*

**Mumm Napa,** 8445 Silverado Trail  Rutherford. This is one of the most fun tasting rooms in the valley, big outdoor patio, and a wonderful photo gallery with both permanent and changing exhibits. The wines are world class, very interesting and innovative.  Great gift shop and the views over the vineyards at sunset are great. Chocolate is always available. **Wines**: They do mostly sparkling wines but their still wines are very good in a crisp, un-oaked style. Hrs: 10-5  TF: $ - $$$  by glass or flight with table service.
***Directions:*** *To return to San Francisco continue south (right) on Silverado to traffic light, Trancas, turn right (coffee shops and fuel) and follow that to the Hwy 29 south entrance.*

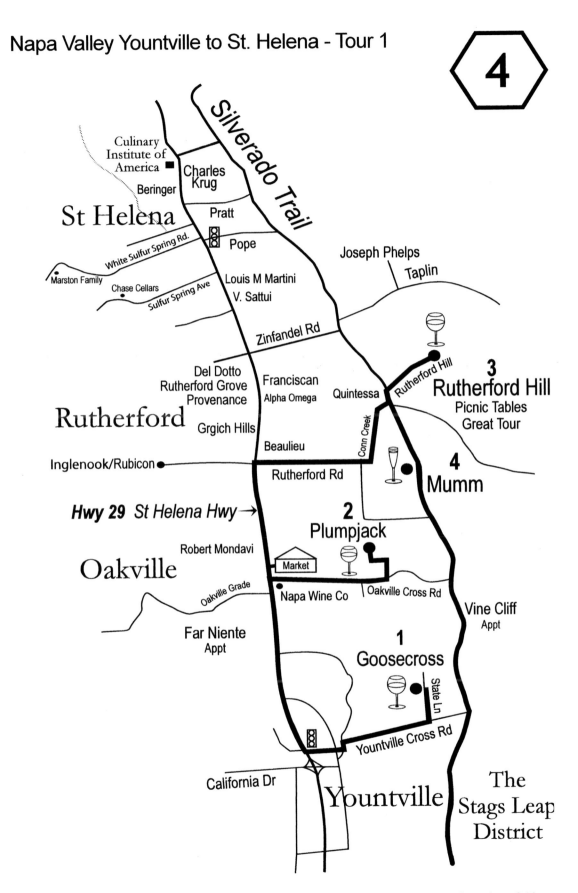

# Tour 2: Great Views, Lovely Gardens, Farms & Italian Style

**Artesa Winery,** 1345 Henry Rd. Napa. This was originally built to make sparkling wines, but when that market slowed they converted to still wines with great success. The winery was built by taking the top of the mountain off, building the winery and then covering it with dirt and grass. From the outside it looks like a bunker, but the views from the inside and patio are spectacular. Take the tour. Hrs: 10-5  TF: $$. **Wines:** They offer Spanish, Bordeaux & Burgundy style wines.

**Directions:** *Backtrack to Hwy 121  and turn left (east) to Hwy 29, turn left (north). Take the Yountville/California Ave exit and bear right to T intersection, turn left to the center of Yountville: 14.9 miles, 25 minutes. Pick up* **picnic** *items at* **Bouchon Bakery, Ranch Market** *or* **NapaStyle.**
**Directions:** *Take Yountville Cross Rd to Cliff Lede: total 2.2 miles.*

**Cliff Lede Vineyards,** 1473 Yountville Cross Rd.  Yountville. This is in the Stags Leap District. A charming small tasting room with a great garden/patio,  art gallery and excellent wines.  Hrs: 10-5 TF: $$-$$$  **Wines:** Bordeaux style.
**Directions:** *Turn right and take Yountville Cross Rd to Silverado Trail, turn right to Regusci Winery, on the left-hand side: 3.5 miles, approx 5 minutes.*

**Regusci Winery,** 5584 Silverado Trail  Napa. They are housed in the oldest winery building in the Stags Leap District. This is a working farm complete with friendly dogs, pick-up trucks and wonderful wines. The staff is casual and informative. With four tastings you can enjoy one of their great picnic tables. Hrs: 10-5  TF: $$$  **Wines:** Cab Sauv, Merlot, Zin, and Chard.
**Directions:** *Turn left to Luna Vineyards, right side: 4 miles,  5 mins.*

**Luna Vineyards,** 2921 Silverado Trail  Napa. This is one of the southernmost wineries on the Silverado Trail. The tasting room is gorgeous, and the sit down tasting room in the back which is arranged by appointment is equally elegant. One of their reasons for being is a love of Italian varietals, which they do quite well, but they also do good Bordeaux style blends. Hrs: 10-5   TF: $$ - $$$.

**Directions:** *To reach pretty much any place, continue south to Trancas and turn right. You can find both coffee and fuel there. In a couple of miles it will bring you to the entrances to Hwy 29.*

# Napa Carneros to Yountville - Tour 2

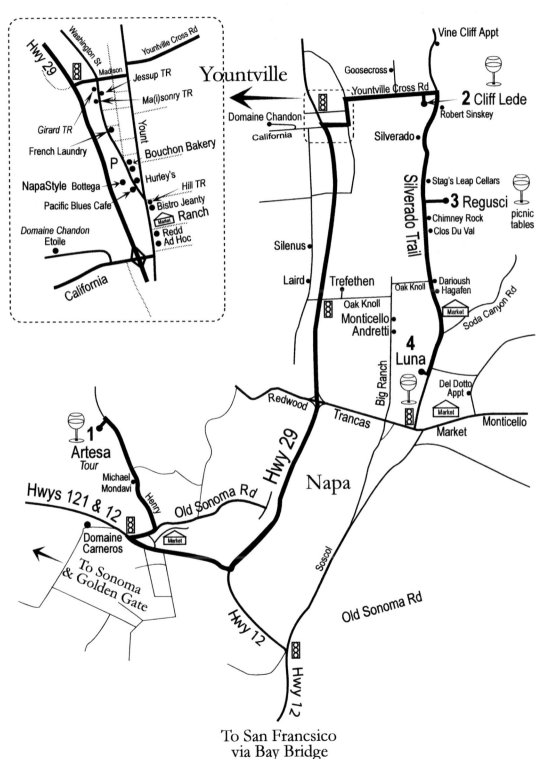

Yountville

**Inset (upper left):**

Hwy 29
Washington St
Yountville Cross Rd
Madison
Jessup TR
Ma(i)sonry TR
Girard TR
Yount
French Laundry
Bouchon Bakery
P
NapaStyle
Bottega
Hurley's
Hill TR
Pacific Blues Cafe
Bistro Jeanty
Market
Ranch
Domaine Chandon
Etoile
Redd
Ad Hoc
California

**Main map:**

Vine Cliff Appt
Goosecross
Yountville Cross Rd
Domaine Chandon
California
**2** Cliff Lede
Robert Sinskey
Silverado
Silverado Trail
Stag's Leap Cellars
**3** Regusci
picnic tables
Chimney Rock
Clos Du Val
Silenus
Laird
Trefethen
Oak Knoll
Darioush
Hagafen
Oak Knoll
Monticello
Andretti
Market
Soda Canyon Rd
Big Ranch
**4** Luna
Del Dotto Appt
Market
Redwood
Trancas
Hwy 29
Monticello
Market
Monticello
Napa
**1** Artesa Tour
Michael Mondavi
Henry
Old Sonoma Rd
Hwys 121 & 12
Domaine Carneros
Market
Soscol
To Sonoma & Golden Gate
Hwy 12
Old Sonoma Rd
Hwy 12

To San Franscico
via Bay Bridge

# Tour 3: Family Wineries with Great Caves and Stories

These wineries produce big, high alcohol red wines. Reynolds is usually just a tasting but they have a tour option. Vine Cliff, with the tour, needs 1.25 hours, although you can just taste. Both are by appointment. From the south go north on Hwy 29, exit at Trancas, bear right to the Silverado Trail, Turn Left.

*Reynolds Family will be on the right side, not far past Luna Vineyards (on the left). If you get to the Soda Canyon Store you went to far,*

*A **Second Market Option**. The Monticello deli is on Trancas/Monticello between the Silverado Trail and Atlas Peak Road. This is a locals favorite. It tends to be less crazed than the Soda Canyon store and the food and service are excellent. There are indoor tables for hot or wet days.*

**Reynolds Family Winery**, 3266 Silverado Trail  Napa. This is a friendly family winery with excellent wines. The tasting room is attached to the winery and next to the vineyards. The staff is knowledgeable & friendly. The patio is a great place to do a tasting and have a bite to eat.  A great tour into the vineyards by **appointment**  Hrs: 10:30-4:30  instant appts  TF: $$  **Wines**: Cab Sauv, Pinot Noir, Chard, a blend called Persistence.

**Directions:** *For lunch stop at the Soda Canyon Market, there are picnic tables out back or arrange for a table with Regusci. Then go north on Silverado Trail, Regusci is on the right side just past Chimney Rock.*

**Regusci Winery**, 5584 Silverado Trail  Napa. They are housed in the oldest winery building in the Stags Leap District. This is a working farm complete with friendly dogs, pick-up trucks and wonderful wines. The staff is casual and informative. With four tastings you can enjoy one of their great picnic tables. Hrs: 10-5  TF: $$$  **Wines**: Cab Sauv, Merlot, Zin, and Chard.
**Directions:** *Turn right to Vine Cliff just past the earthen dam on the right. At the gate, push the call buttons. 10 minutes.*

**Vine Cliff Winery,** 7400 Silverado Trail  Yountville. This is a favorite. A jewel of a winery in its own canyon. A great tour, beautiful caves, wonderful wines, surrounded by unique gardens. The staff is very friendly and informative. Call for an **appointment**, even last minute, 707.944.1364,  Hrs: 10-5.  TF: $$$  **Wines**: Cab Sauv, Chard, Merlot.

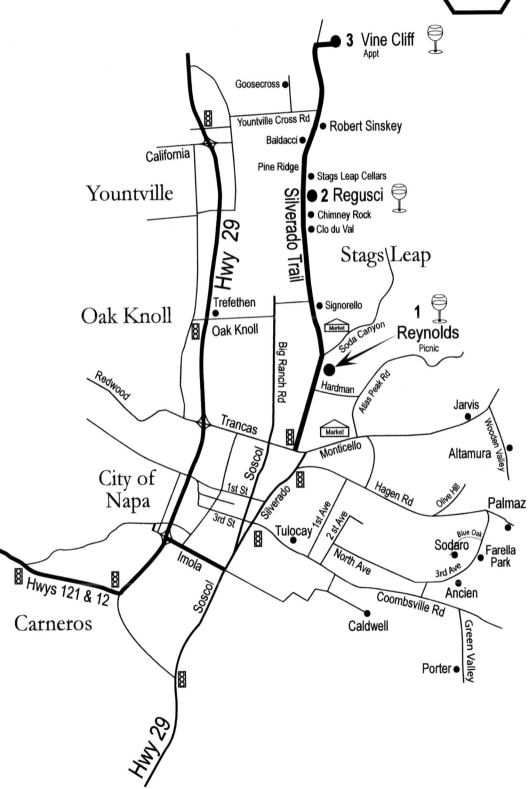

# Tour 4: Charming Napa + Two Appointments

**Cakebread Cellars,** 8300 St Helena Hwy (Hwy 29) Rutherford. One of America's favorite restaurant wines, surrounded by vines. ***Navigation Hint:*** Going north, they are on the right side past Turnbull and before Sequoia Grove. The only signs are the small blue and white ones on the road and their name on the mailbox. Call for an ***appointment:*** 800.588.0298, and be 10 minutes early. Hrs: 10-4  TF: $$ - $$$  **Wines:** Sauv Blanc, Chard, Pinot Noir, Merlot, Syrah, Zin, Cab Sauv, Rubaiyat.
***Directions:*** *North to Rutherford Road, turn right. At the intersection with Conn Creek & Skellenger bear left. Frog's Leap is on the left in a big Red barn with a leaping frog weathervane. A small sign is on the white fence rail.*

**Frog's Leap Winery,** 8815 Conn Creek Rd.  Rutherford. They are one of the greenest organic wineries in Napa. Their new hospitality center is a delight. They also do tastings in the garden and in the barn loft, Very cool! Hrs:10-4 TF: $$$  **Wines:** Merlot, Zin, Chard, Sauv Blanc, Cab Sauv, Syrah, Blends.
***Lunch Directions:*** *Return to Hwy 29, turn right (North) to Dean & DeLuca on the left-hand side, or V. Sattui (1111 White Ln., St. Helena ) on the right side: total 3.3 miles, approx 5 minutes*
***Directions:*** *South to Zinfandel Ln, turn left to Kelham Vineyards on left side: total 1.3 miles, approx 2 minutes*

**Kelham Winery** 360 Zinfandel Ln., St. Helena    This is a fantastic family winery that makes great Bordeaux style wines that are poured by the winemakers and owners. A personal favorite. ***By Appointment.*** Hours: 10-5
Tasting Fee:$$$$$ **Wines:** Cab Sauv, Sauv Blanc, Merlot, Chard
***Safety Hint:*** Only consider going to one more winery if you have a designated driver or professional driver/guide, because these three offer serious tastings.
 ***Directions:*** *Turn left to Silverado Trail, right to the Yountville Cross Rd. Turn right. At the stop sign turn left. At the next stop turn right. At the next stop sign turn left onto Washington. Follow that through town. At California (a stop sign) turn right and go under the highway. Domaine Chandon will be on the right.*

**Domaine Chandon**, 1 California Dr. Yountville. They are a well-known producer of sparkling wines with a large, gracious winery with expansive grounds, big tasting room and patio. Nice tours and a great gift shop. Also home to the restaurant Etoile. Hrs: 10-5   TF: $$ & by the glass.  **Wines:** A wide variety of sparkling and still wines.

# Central Napa Valley - Tour 4

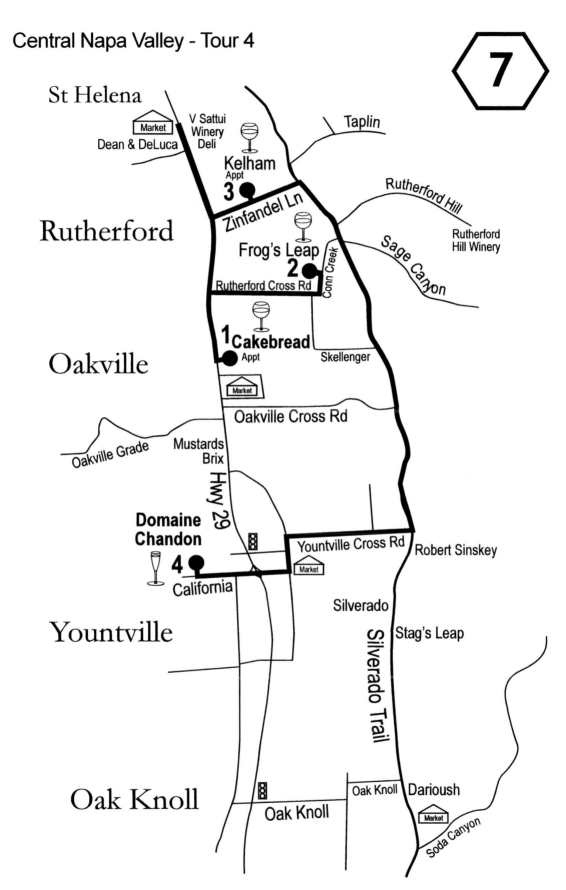

St Helena

V Sattui
Winery
Deli

Market

Dean & DeLuca

Kelham
Appt
**3**

Taplin

Zinfandel Ln

Rutherford Hill

Rutherford

Frog's Leap
**2**

Rutherford Cross Rd

Conn Creek

Sage Canyon

Rutherford
Hill Winery

**1** Cakebread
Appt

Skellenger

Oakville

Market

Oakville Cross Rd

Oakville Grade

Mustards
Brix

Hwy 29

**Domaine
Chandon**

**4**

California

Yountville Cross Rd

Market

Robert Sinskey

Silverado

Stag's Leap

Silverado Trail

Yountville

Oak Knoll

Oak Knoll

Oak Knoll

Darioush

Market

Soda Canyon

Tours, Overviews & Maps

# Tour 5: Golden Gate, Sparkling Carneros, Views & Dreams

**Domaine Carneros,** 1240 Duhig Rd.  Napa. They are perched on a hill in sight of Carneros Highway. This is a well-known landmark and a popular winery. Great views, wonderful staff, classic French style building, nice tour and gifts, and world class sparkling wines.   Hrs: 10-6  TF: $$. Table service by the glass or flight.
**Directions:** *Follow Hwy 121 to Hwy 29 (A traffic light), turn left and follow this to Oakville. The entrance to Opus One is just past the* **Oakville Market**. *Stop in and pick up sandwiches before the rush. Opus One is styled like an Aztec temple and the big gate has a small sign, but the building is hard to miss.*

**Opus One Winery,** 7900 St. Helena Hwy (*Hwy* 29)  Oakville. They are a world standard, making 25,000 cases a year, and the current bottle price is above $180. While there are plenty of Napa wines of comparable quality and price, few are more famous than this joint dream of Robert Mondavi and Baron Phillipe Von Rothschild.  Hrs: 10-4  Call for appointment (707.944.9442), but instant appts can be arranged outside of the high season. Tours are always by appointment and very cool! TF: $$$$  **Wines:** Bordeaux style Blend.
**Directions:** *To reach Silverado Vineyards, go out the driveway on the right side of the Opus building. The gate will open as you approach it. At Oakville Cross Rd. turn left to Silverado Trail. Turn right and Silverado will be 1/2 mile past the turn for the Yountville Cross Road on the right side. It has tremendous views. 5.6 miles, 12 minutes.*

**Silverado Vineyards,** 6121 Silverado Trail  Napa. They are perched on a hill in the Stags Leap District. A beautiful Spanish-style winery with great views, a lovely patio, good wines and a friendly staff.  Owned by the Disney Family.
Hrs: 10:30-4:30 TF: $$ - $$$ **Wines:** Bordeaux, Burgundy, Italian varietals.
**Directions:** *Turn right out the driveway, Darioush will be on the left side just past the turn for Oak Knoll Ave. 4 miles, 5 minutes.*

**Darioush,** 4240 Silverado Trail  Napa. This is a stunning winery and grounds just south of the Stags Leap District, well known for good Bordeaux, Burgundy and Rhone varietals. A beautiful, pricey gift shop. Hrs: 10:30-5  TF: $$$.
**Directions:** *To reach pretty much any place, continue south to Trancas and turn right. You can find both coffee and fuel there. In a couple of miles it will bring you to the entrances to Hwy 29.*

# From Carneros Napa to Oakville - Tour 5

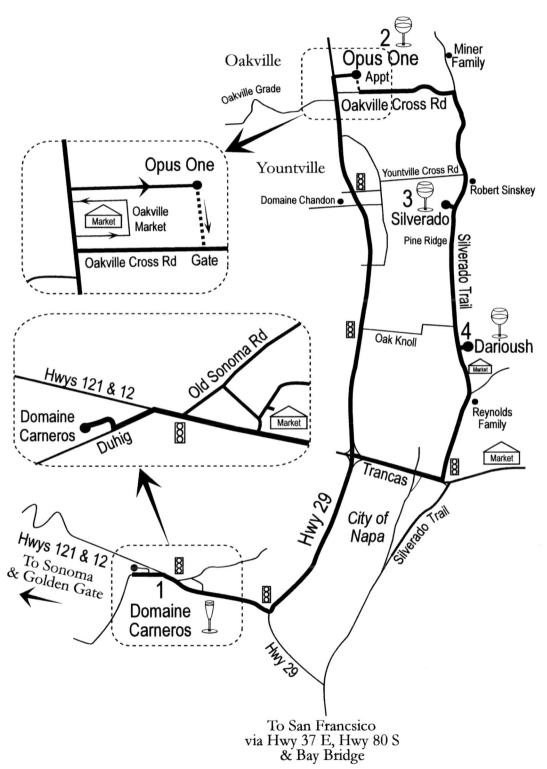

Oakville

**2**
**Opus One**
Appt

Miner Family

Oakville Grade

Oakville Cross Rd

Opus One

Market
Oakville Market

Oakville Cross Rd        Gate

Yountville

Yountville Cross Rd

Domaine Chandon

Robert Sinskey

**3**
**Silverado**

Pine Ridge

Silverado Trail

Old Sonoma Rd

Hwys 121 & 12

Domaine Carneros        Duhig

Market

Oak Knoll

**4**
Darioush

Market

Reynolds Family

Market

Trancas

City of Napa

Hwy 29

Silverado Trail

Hwys 121 & 12
To Sonoma & Golden Gate

**1**
**Domaine Carneros**

Hwy 29

To San Francsico
via Hwy 37 E, Hwy 80 S
& Bay Bridge

# Tour 6: Serious Red Wines & a Wonderful Rutherford Day

Cabernet is King in Napa and these wineries are famous for big red Bordeaux-style wines. Stag's Leap Cellars is famous for its win at the 1976 Judgment of Paris that compared French and American wines. Silver Oak is popular for their warm flavored, American oak barrels and extensive aging, producing a wine ready to drink the day it is sold. Joseph Phelps has a great reputation among serious red wine fans for their wonderful wines that continue to please. Joseph Phelps is by appointment. Rearrange the tour as needed and choose one or the other to make the schedule work. Drink lots of water on this tour because these are high alcohol wines with huge, dehydrating tannins.

**Stag's Leap Wine Cellars,** 5766 Silverado Trail  Napa. One of the Judgment of Paris winners located in the heart of the same named district. They offer regular & reserve tastings in the tasting room and patio. This is a great winery to visit on a corporate group tour since it takes you into their wonderful caves. Hrs: 10-4:30 TF: $$ - $$$  **Wines**: Sauv Blanc, Chard, Merlot, Cab Sauv.
*Directions: Turn right to Oakville Cross Rd, turn left to Silver Oak which will be on the left-hand side: total 5.9 miles, approx 8 minutes.*

**Silver Oak Cellars,** 915 Oakville Cross Rd.  Oakville. They pour two big Cab Sauv blends from Napa and Alexander Valley, Sonoma. They completely, and beautifully transformed their site recently. Friendly, casual staff. Hrs: 9-5, Sunday 11-5, TF: $$  **Wines**: Cab Sauv blends from Napa and Alexander Valley, Sonoma.
*Directions: Turn left to Hwy 29, turn right and the* **Oakville Grocery** *is immediately on the right side, pull into parking lot and enjoy a picnic lunch.*
*Directions: Turn right on Hwy 29, at Zinfandel Rd turn right. At the intersection with Silverado Trail turn left. Taplin Rd, will be on the right. This is a narrow but short drive to the obvious Phelps sign on the left.*

**Joseph Phelps Vineyards,** 200 Taplin Rd  St. Helena. The first Napa winery to create a Bordeaux-style blend. Tucked in their own valley they offer wonderful  tastings and seminars by ***appointment:*** 707.967.3720. Lovely tasting room & patio, very knowledgeable and relaxed staff. Beautiful building. They offer some of the best winery based seminars in the valley. Check their site. Hrs: appt  9-5 Mon-Fri  Sat/Sun 10-4  TF: $$$ - $$$$  **Wines**: Bordeaux, Rhone. **Note**: Phelps has picnic tables available to wine club members, and sometimes others. Inquire when you call to see if one is available.

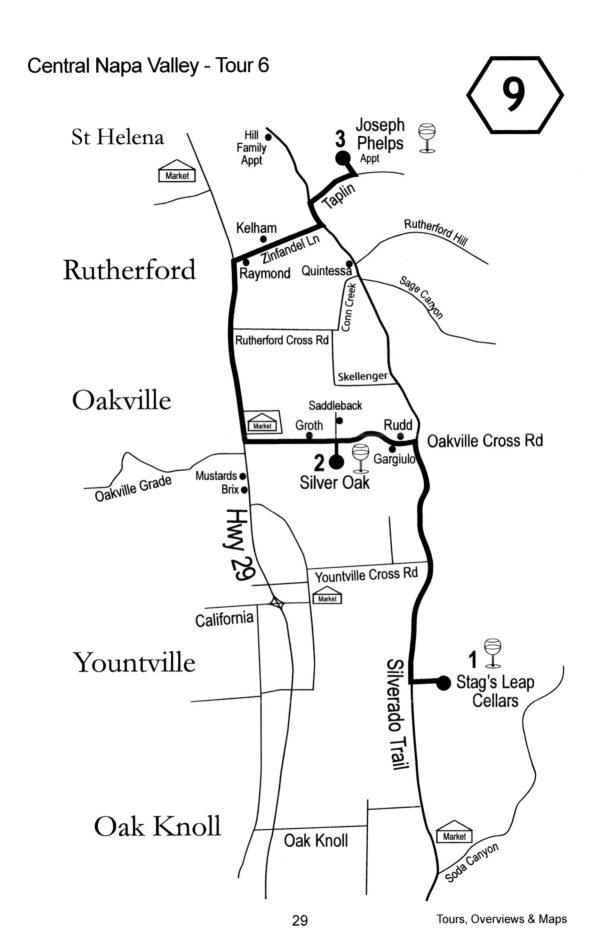

# Overview 1: Destination Wineries in Northern Napa

**Beringer Vineyards,** 2000 Main St. (Hwy 29) St. Helena. Continuously running since 1876, they offer an amazing variety of tours and both standard (in the old winery) and reserve (in the Mansion) tastings. A beautiful, historic winery surrounded by lovely, gracious grounds. Don't miss it! Hrs: 10-5 Tours TF: $$ - $$$. **Wines:** Too numerous to list. You name it, they have it!

**Castello di Amorosa,** 4045 N. St Helena Hwy (Hwy 29) Calistoga. Modeled on a composite of 12th century Tuscan castles, complete with dungeon. Guided & self-guided tours. Cool in the winter, but great in the Summer. Big tasting room/gift shop and fun staff. The views from the ramparts are great. Hrs: 9-6, 9-5 Nov-Feb TF: $$$ - $$$$ **Wines:** A dozen wines from dry to sweet.

**Chateau Montelena Winery,** 1429 Tubbs Ln. Calistoga. Famous for their winning chardonnay at the 1976 Judgment of Paris that made Napa wines famous & inspired the movie Bottle Shock. A gorgeous building from the 1800's with remarkable grounds and a beautiful lake. TF: $$ - $$$$ Hrs: 9:30-4 **Wines:** Chardonnay, Cabernet Sauvignon, Zinfandel, Riesling.

**Clos Pegase Winery,** 1060 Dunaweal Ln. Calistoga. A great art collection, incredible building and eclectic tasting room. Free guided tours at 11 & 2. Hrs: 10:30-5 TF: $$ - $$$ Picnic tables near the fountains. **Wines:** Chard, Sauv Blanc, Pinot Noir, Merlot, Cab Sauv.

**Schramsberg Vineyards,** 1400 Schramsberg Rd. Calistoga. These are the oldest mountainside caves in Napa. The scheduled tour includes a tasting and it's worth the effort of fitting it into your schedule. By *appointment:* 707.942.2414, Hrs: 10-4 TF: $$$ **Wines:** Various sparkling wines, Cab Sauv.

**Spring Mountain Vineyards,** 2805 Spring Mountain Rd. St. Helena. The biggest estate on Spring Mountain, it was used in the TV series Falcon Crest. Wonderful staff and great wines. Allow 2 hours for the cave/mansion tour. Call for an *appointment:* 707.967.4188. Hrs: 10-5, Tasting & Tour Fee: $$$ (applied to purchase) **Wines:** Syrah, Cab Sauv, Sauv Blanc.

**Sterling Vineyards,** 1111 Dunaweal Ln. Calistoga. This winery sits on top of a hill and is reached via tramway. It is a fun time, with a good gift shop, great views & tours. Allow 2 hours. In the busy season go early, the tram seats can get hot! Hrs: 10:30-4 TF: $$$ **Wines:** Cab Sauv, Merlot, Chard, Pinot Noir, Shiraz, Sauv Blanc, Blends.

Storybook Mountain

Bennett Lane

Atalon

Bennett Ln

**Chateau Montelena**

Hans Fahden

Summers

Tubbs Ln

Vincent Arroyo

Envy

Greenwood

Petrified Forest Rd

Calistoga

Zahtila

August Briggs

Market

Lava

Vermeil

Lincoln

Von Strasser

Reverie

Diamond Mtn Rd

Constant Diamond

**Clos Pegase**

Picnic

Dunaweal Ln

Hwy 29

Twomey

**Sterling**

Cuvaison

Picnic

Dutch Henry

Paoletti

Larkmead Ln

Welcome to Napa Sign

**Castello di Amorosa**

Appt for Tour

Larkmead

Picnic

Scherwin Family

Barnett

**Frank Family**

Wermuth

Pride Mountain

Smith Madrone

**Schramsburg**

Appt

Bale Ln

Silverado Trail

Charbay

Schweiger

Benessere

Big Tree

Tudal

Paloma

V Madrone

Ehlers Ln

Allora

Ehlers

Terra Valentine

Robert Keenan

**Rombauer**

Failla

School House

**Trinchero**

Picnic

Casa Nuestra

Chateau Boswell

Cain

Freemark Abbey

Stony Hill

A Dozen Vintners

Vineyard 29

St Clement

Lodi

Duckhorn

Revana

Ballentine

Markham

**Spring Mountain**

Appointment

**Culinary Institute of America**

Deer Park

Charles Krug

Pratt

**Beringer**

Pope

Market

Merryvale

St Helena

# Overview 2: Favorite Wineries in Northern Napa

**Benessere Vineyards,** 1010 Big Tree Rd. St. Helena. This is a romantic jewel of a winery, intimate with a friendly staff on a pretty site a distance off the road. They specialize in Italian varietals, but they include other types as well. The tasting room is attached to the winery. There are a few small *picnic* tables under the rose arbor that you can enjoy. Hrs: 10-5 TF: $$ **Wines**: Pinot Grigio, Sangiovese, Syrah, Zin, Pinot Noir, Muscat di Canelli, Blends.

**Failla,** 3530 Silverado Trail St. Helena. They make some of the best Pinot Noir and Chardonnay in Napa because the grapes come from Sonoma's Coastal region. They have great winery caves, a wonderful staff in a charming bungalow tasting room. Call for an *appointment:* 707.963.0530 Hrs: 10-5 by TF: $$ **Wines**: Pinot Noir, Viognier, Syrah, Chard.

**Frank Family Vineyards,** 1091 Larkmead Ln. Calistoga. This historic site recently went through a major transformation for the better, resulting in a beautiful tasting room surrounded by spacious grounds including *picnic* tables. Great wines, fun staff, a north valley favorite among those in the know. Hrs: 10-4 TF: $ **Wines**: Sangiovese, Zin , Cab Sauv, Chard, Sparklers, Zin Port.

**Reverie Vineyard & Winery,** 1520 Diamond Mountain Rd. Calistoga. They start their tasting outside by the tanks, then they move into the caves, and out to a fairy circle of Redwood Trees. The wines are great, the staff is very knowledgeable and the owner/winemaker is often around. It is a beautiful location. They often run out of wine by the end of the season, they are very good, so call for an *appointment:* 707.942.6800 Hrs: 10-5 TF: $$ **Wines**: Cab Franc, Cab Sauv, Sauv Blanc, Barbera, Rousanne.

**St. Clement Vineyards,** 2867 N. St Helena Hwy (Hwy 29) St. Helena. They are housed in a Victorian house overlooking Highway 29 that was built in the late 1800's. It has cute gifts and great views. *Call ahead:* 800.331.8266, to *reserve* one of their wonderful *picnic* tables on the patio out front. Hrs: 10-4 TF: $$ - $$$ **Wines**: Cab Sauv, Merlot, Sauv Blanc, Chard, Syrah.

**Summers Estate Wines,** 1171 Tubbs Ln. Calistoga. This is a pretty family winery near the Old Faithful Geyser. Wonderful wines, friendly, informative staff, a nice gift shop and they have *picnic* tables. Hrs: 10:30-4:30 TF: $$ **Wines**: Cab Sauv, Chard, Merlot, Charbono, Zin, Muscat Canelli, Petite Sirah.

Route 128

Atalon
Bennett
Lane

Bennett Ln

Chateau
Montelena

**Summers**

Tubbs Ln

Vincent
Arroyo

Greenwood

Zahtila

Calistoga

Petrified Forest Rd

Graeser

**Reverie**

Von Strasser

Constant Diamond

Diamond Mtn Rd

August
Briggs    Market

Vermeil

Lincoln

B Cellars

Clos Pegase

Dunaweal Ln

Sterling

Twomey

Cuvaison

Dutch Henry

Paoletti

Hwy 29

Castello
di Amorosa

Larkmead

Larkmead

**Frank
Family**

Wermuth

Scherwin Family    Barnett

Smith Madrone

Pride Mountain

Charbay

Schweiger

Paloma

Robert
Keenan

Terra Valentine

Cain

School
House

Spring Mountain Road

Spring Mountain

Schramsburg

Bale Ln

**Benessere**

Stony Hill

Big Tree

Tudal

Ehlers Ln

Ehlers

**Failla**

**Rombauer**

Trinchero    Casa Nuestra

Freemark Abbey

Lodi

Ballentine

Revana
Ballentine
Markham

Duckhorn

Chateau Boswell

**St Clement**

Deer Park

Beringer

Charles
Krug

**Pratt**

Silverado Trail

Pope

**St Helena**    Market    Merryvale

# Overview 3: Favorite Spring Mountain Wineries

**Barnett Vineyards,** 4070 Spring Mountain Rd. St. Helena. This is a charming family winery that clings to the side of Spring Mountain and produces spectacular wines. Incredible views, excellent staff and ask if you can bring a *picnic,* if that's the time you get there. Make your *appointment:* 707.963.7075, in advance so you don't miss out. Hrs: 10-4   TF: $$$$   **Wines**: Cab Sauv, Pinot Noir, Chard.

**Newton Vineyard,** 2555 Madrona Ave. St. Helena. They do their tastings and tours by *appointment:* 707.963.9000, at 11:00 am, except Mondays. They adjust this with the season. It is a remarkable estate with beautiful architecture and gardens. The views from the ridges of Spring Mountain are incredible, so bring a camera. TF: $$$   **Wines**: Chard, Merlot, Cab Sauv, Cab Franc, Petit Verdot.

**Pride Mountain Vineyards,** 4026 Spring Mountain Rd.  St. Helena. This is at the top of Spring Mountain on the Napa-Sonoma line. A beautiful tasting room, caves, diverse vineyards, great wines and spectacular views. One of the best *picnic* areas in Napa. When you make your appointment ask if you can bring a picnic. If they say yes, they'll direct you to the best site. By *appointment:* 707.963.4949  Hrs: 11-3:30   Mon-Wed-Sat (check their website since this changes), TF: $$ **Wines**: Merlot, Cab Sauv, Cab Franc, Viognier, Chard.

**Schweiger Vineyards,** 4015 Spring Mountain Rd.  St. Helena. They are in a beautiful location and the tastings are downstairs in the barrel room. The family has grown grapes here for many years and produces some wonderful wines. *Appointment:* 707.963.4882, Hrs: 11-4   TF: $$  **Wines**: Sauv Blanc, Chard, Merlot, Cab Sauv, Petite Sirah, Port, blends.

**Terra Valentine,** 3787 Spring Mountain Rd. St. Helena. This winery is housed in an extraordinary, hand-made building, filled with unique art and eccentric features. There is quite a story behind it. The fact that the wines and the staff are great too is an added bonus. Well worth the ride! The tasting includes the tour and is by *appointment:* 707.967.8340  Hrs: by appt TF: $$$   CWP **Wines**: Pinot Noir, Cab Sauv, Bordeaux Blends.

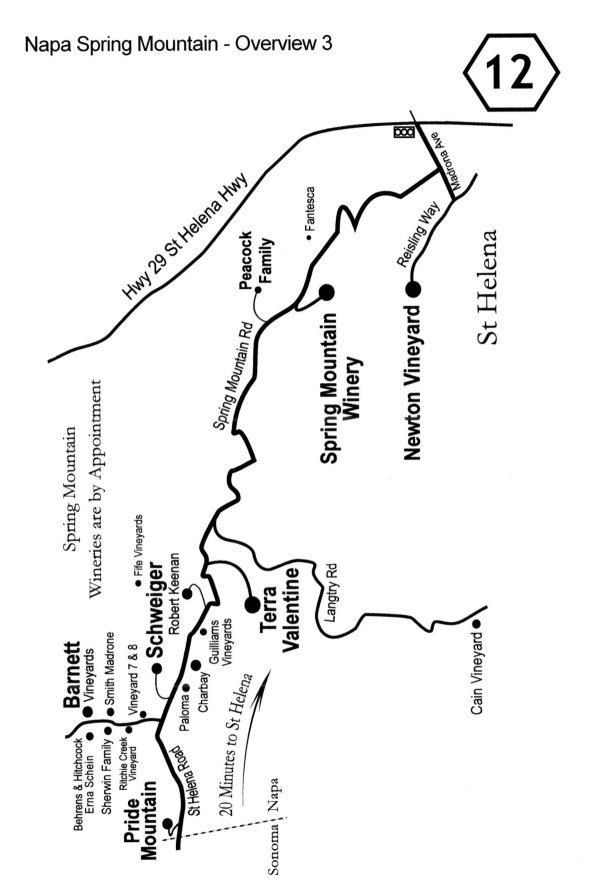

Hwy 29 St Helena Hwy

Spring Mountain Rd

Peacock Family

• Fantesca

Madrona Ave

Reisling Way

St Helena

Spring Mountain Winery

Newton Vineyard

Spring Mountain
Wineries are by Appointment

• Fife Vineyards

Schweiger

Robert Keenan

Langtry Rd

Terra Valentine

Barnett
Vineyards

• Smith Madrone

Vineyard 7 & 8

Guilliams Vineyards

Charbay

Paloma

Cain Vineyard

Behrens & Hitchcock
Erna Schein

Sherwin Family

Ritchie Creek
Vineyard

Pride Mountain

St Helena Road

20 Minutes to St Helena

Sonoma    Napa

# Overview 4: Deer Park, Howell Mountain & Conn Valley

These warm vineyards in the volcanic Vaca Mountains are known for big, strong Bordeaux-style reds with great aging potential. Allow two hours per visit, and go with the intention of buying wine. *Howell Mountain Road between Conn Valley Road and White Cottage Road is very narrow and winding. Avoid it, especially with passengers in the back seat! The best plan is to hire a guide.*

**Bremer Family Winery,** 975 Deer Park Rd. St. Helena. This is a friendly winery where the tastings are done outside in the nice weather (max party of 6 inside in Winter). Hrs: 10-5  TF: $  Call for an ***appointment:*** 707.963.5411  **Wines**: Cab Sauv, Merlot, Zin, Cab Franc, Claret, Petite Sirah, Port, White Port.

**Cade Winery,** 360 Howell Mountain Rd. S. Angwin. A state of the art winery with spectacular views and caves owned by Plumpjack. Hrs: by ***appointment:*** 707.945.1220  TF: $$  with Tours, **Wines**: Cab blend, Sauv Blanc, Semillon.

**Ladera,** 150 White Cottage Rd. S. Angwin. One of the most historic winery buildings on Howell with neat tours. Hrs: by ***appointment:*** 707.965.2445  TF: $$ - $$$  **Wines**: Cab Sauv, Sauv Blanc, Malbec.

**Viader,** 1120 Deer Park Rd  Deer Park. This is a popular family run, high end winery with food pairings and dining by *appointment*. Hrs: 10-4:30 by ***appointment:*** 707.963.3816  TF: $$$$  **Wines**: Bordeaux style, Syrah, Tempranillo.

**White Cottage Ranch Winery,** 555 College Ave.  Angwin. This is local family owned, and run winery on a pretty site.  Hrs: by ***appointment:*** 707.965.0516 **Wines**: Sauv Blanc, Chard, Merlot, Cab Sauv, Cab Franc, Sangiovese, Zin, Syrah.

## Lower Howell Mountain Road and Conn Valley

**Anderson's Conn Valley Vineyards,** 680 Rossi Rd.  St. Helena. This is a friendly, casual winery with interesting caves and very good wines. When you fit them into your day, set your time limits because their tour can run long. Nice *picnic* site. Hrs: by ***appointment:*** 707.963.8600, same day appts.  TF: PIE **Wines**: Cab Sauv, Pinot Noir, Blends: Éloge, Éloge Gold, Right Bank, Chard.

**Forman Vineyards,** 1501 Big Rock Rd.  St. Helena. This is tucked away in its own canyon down a steep road in a cute little building, wonderful wines. Ric Forman was the founding winemaker at Sterling. Hrs: by ***appointment:*** 707.963.3900  TF: PIE  **Wines**: Cab Blend, Chard.

Aetna Springs

Pope Valley Winery

Pope Valley

Howell Mountain Road

Ink Grade Rd

Summit Lake
Lamborn
Robert Foley

Outpost

Summit Lake Dr

White Cottage Rd

Howell Mountain Road

Dunn

Friesen Dr

White Cottage

O'Shaughnessy

Buckeye Ln →

College Ave

Neal Family

Liparita Ave

Angwin

Brookside

Ladera

Bravante

Cade

West Lane

White Cottage Rd

Howell Mountain Road

Viader
Burgess

Every Winery Here
is by Appointment

Broman
Bremer

Deer Park Rd

Sanatarium Rd

Very Winding and Narrow
Howell Mountain Road South

Amizetta

Anderson's
Conn Valley

Hwy 29 St Helena Hwy

Deer Park

Silverado Trail

Foreman

Big Rock Rd

Conn Valley Rd

Rossi Rd

Buehler

Howell Mountain Rd

Seavey

Tours, Overviews & Maps

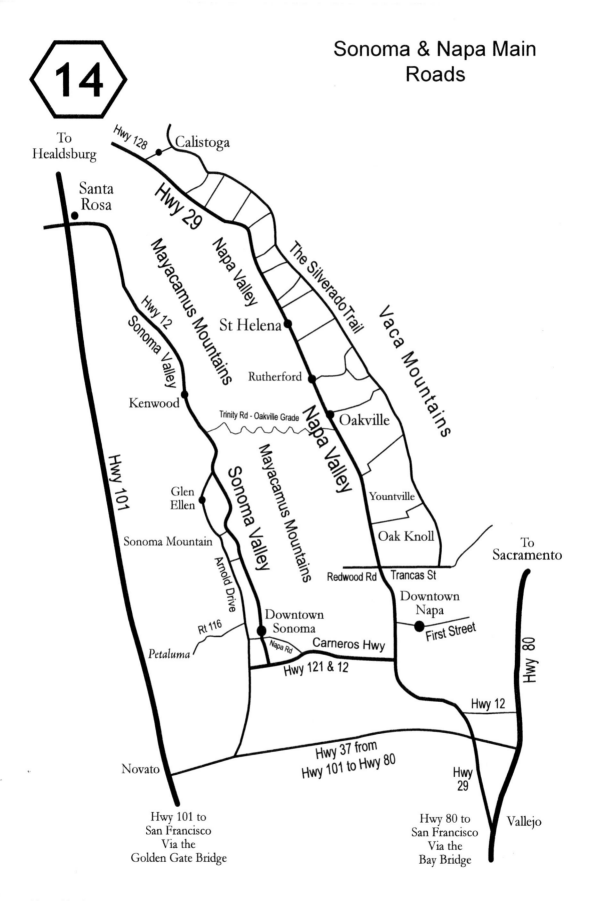

Sonoma & Napa Main Roads

14

# Los Carneros

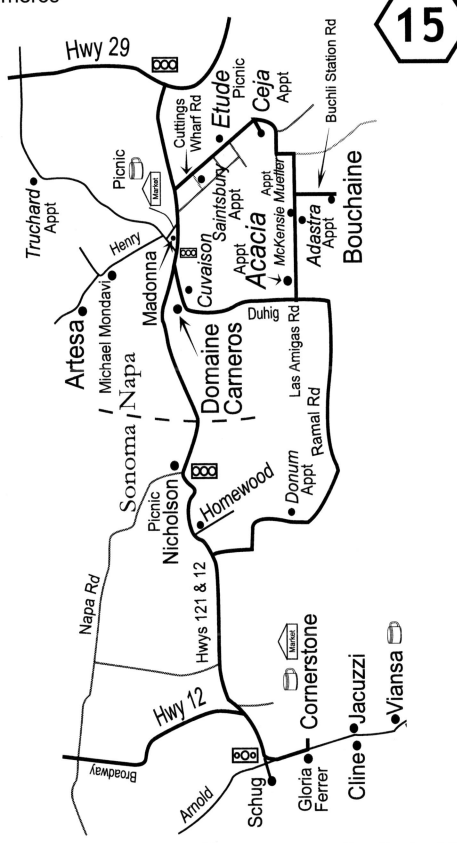

Hwy 29

Truchard Appt

Picnic

Market

Cuttings Wharf Rd

Etude

Picnic

Ceja Appt

Buchli Station Rd

Henry

Madonna

Cuvaison Appt

Saintsbury Appt

Acacia Appt

McKensie Mueller Appt

Adastra Appt

Bouchaine

Artesa

Michael Mondavi

Napa

Domaine Carneros

Duhig

Las Amigas Rd

Sonoma

Napa Rd

Picnic

Nicholson

Homewood

Donum Appt

Ramal Rd

Hwys 121 & 12

Market

Cornerstone

Jacuzzi

Cline

Viansa

Hwy 12

Broadway

Arnold

Schug

Gloria Ferrer

Tours, Overviews & Maps

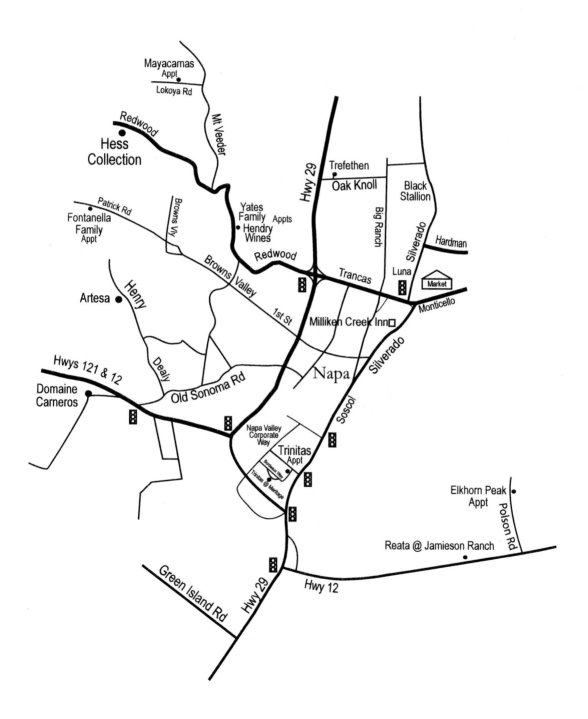

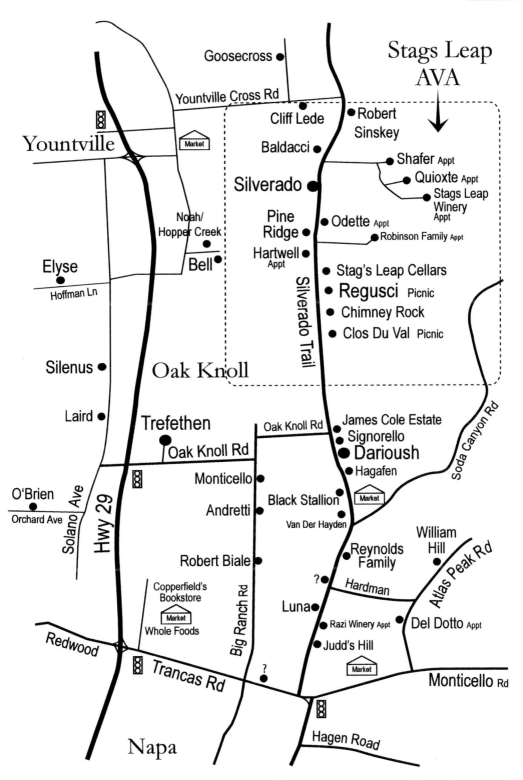

Stags Leap
AVA

Goosecross •

Yountville Cross Rd

Cliff Lede    • Robert
Sinskey

Yountville    Market

Baldacci •

Silverado •    • Shafer Appt
• Quioxte Appt
Pine    • Stags Leap
Ridge    • Odette Appt    Winery
Appt
Noah/
Hopper Creek    • Robinson Family Appt

Elyse •    Hartwell •
Appt
Bell •    • Stag's Leap Cellars
Hoffman Ln    • Regusci    Picnic

• Chimney Rock

• Clos Du Val    Picnic

Silenus •    Oak Knoll

Silverado Trail

Laird •    Oak Knoll Rd    • James Cole Estate
Trefethen    • Signorello
• Darioush
Oak Knoll Rd

O'Brien    Monticello •    • Hagafen
Orchard Ave    Market
Black Stallion •
Andretti •    Soda Canyon Rd
Van Der Hayden •

William
Hill
Reynolds    •
Robert Biale •    Family
? •    Hardman
Copperfield's
Bookstore    Luna •    • Del Dotto Appt
Market    • Razi Winery Appt
Whole Foods    • Judd's Hill    Market
Redwood    Big Ranch Rd
Trancas Rd    ? •    Monticello Rd
Atlas Peak Rd

Hwy 29    Solano Ave

Napa    Hagen Road

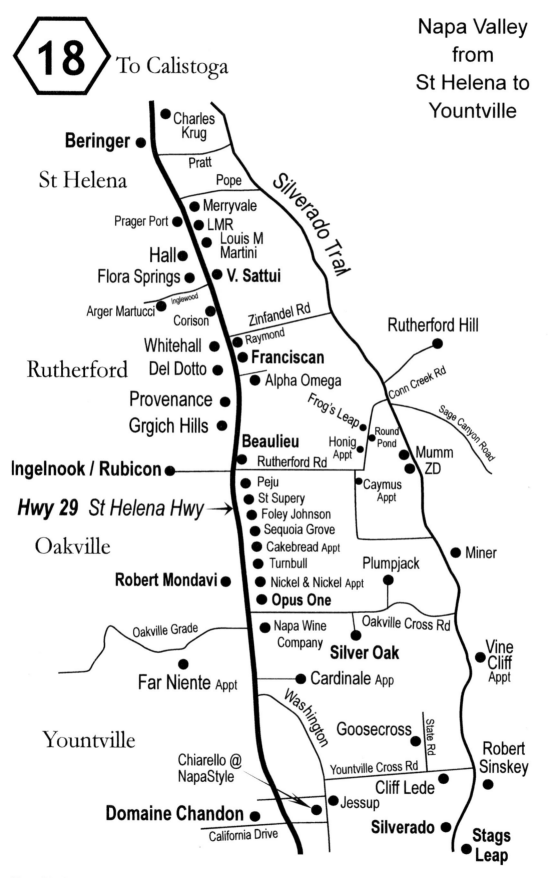

Charles Krug

**Beringer** ●

St Helena

Pratt

Pope

Silverado Trail

● Merryvale

Prager Port ● ● LMR

● Louis M Martini

**Hall** ●

Flora Springs ● ● **V. Sattui**

Inglewood

Arger Martucci ●

Corison

Zinfandel Rd

● Raymond

Whitehall ● **Franciscan**

Rutherford

Del Dotto ● ● Alpha Omega

Rutherford Hill ●

Provenance ●

Grgich Hills ●

Conn Creek Rd

Sage Canyon Road

Frog's Leap

**Beaulieu**

Round Pond

Rutherford Rd

Honig Appt

**Ingelnook / Rubicon** ●

Mumm ZD

● Peju

*Hwy 29  St Helena Hwy* →

● St Supery

Caymus Appt

● Foley Johnson

● Sequoia Grove

Oakville

● Cakebread Appt

Miner ●

● Turnbull

Plumpjack

**Robert Mondavi** ●

● Nickel & Nickel Appt

● **Opus One**

Oakville Cross Rd

Oakville Grade

● Napa Wine Company

**Silver Oak**

Vine Cliff Appt

Far Niente Appt

● **Cardinale** App

Washington

Goosecross

State Rd

Robert Sinskey

Yountville

Chiarello @ NapaStyle

Yountville Cross Rd

Cliff Lede

● Jessup

**Domaine Chandon** ●

**Silverado** ●

**Stags Leap**

California Drive

# From Domaine Chandon to V. Sattui

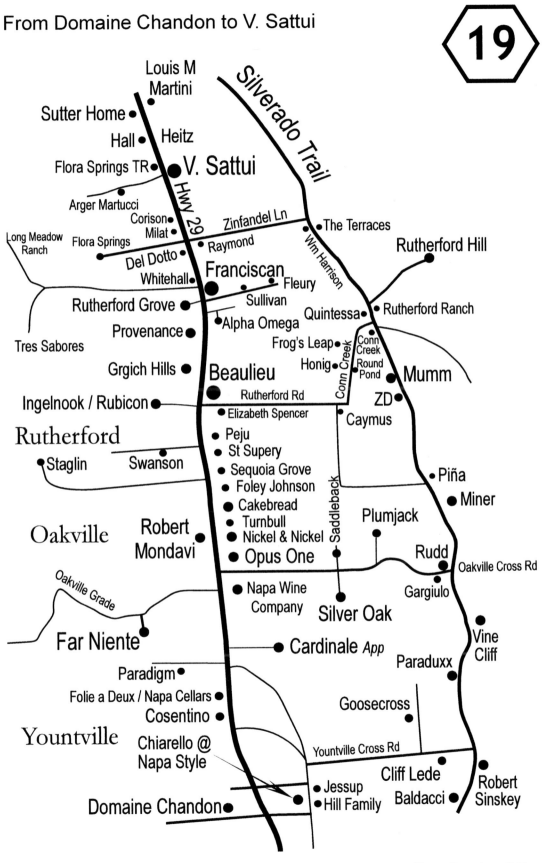

Louis M Martini
Sutter Home
Hall
Heitz
Flora Springs TR
V. Sattui
Silverado Trail
Arger Martucci
Corison
Milat
Zinfandel Ln
The Terraces
Long Meadow Ranch
Flora Springs
Raymond
Del Dotto
Wm Harrison
Rutherford Hill
Whitehall
Franciscan
Fleury
Hwy 29
Rutherford Grove
Sullivan
Alpha Omega
Quintessa
Rutherford Ranch
Provenance
Frog's Leap
Conn Creek
Tres Sabores
Honig
Round Pond
Grgich Hills
Beaulieu
Conn Creek
Mumm
Ingelnook / Rubicon
Rutherford Rd
ZD
Rutherford
Elizabeth Spencer
Caymus
Peju
St Supery
Staglin
Swanson
Sequoia Grove
Foley Johnson
Saddleback
Piña
Miner
Cakebread
Turnbull
Plumjack
Oakville
Robert Mondavi
Nickel & Nickel
Opus One
Rudd
Oakville Cross Rd
Oakville Grade
Napa Wine Company
Gargiulo
Silver Oak
Far Niente
Cardinale App
Vine Cliff
Paradigm
Paraduxx
Folie a Deux / Napa Cellars
Goosecross
Cosentino
Yountville
Chiarello @ Napa Style
Yountville Cross Rd
Cliff Lede
Jessup
Baldacci
Robert Sinskey
Domaine Chandon
Hill Family

Tours, Overviews & Maps

# Napa Sage Canyon, & Chiles Valley

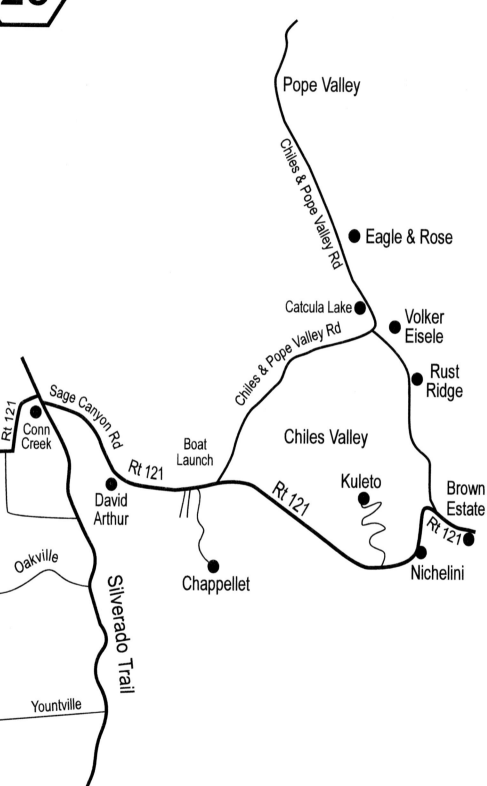

Pope Valley

Chiles & Pope Valley Rd

● Eagle & Rose

Catcula Lake ●

Volker
Eisele

● Rust
Ridge

Chiles & Pope Valley Rd

Rt 121

Sage Canyon Rd

Conn
Creek

Rt 121

Boat
Launch

Chiles Valley

David
Arthur

Kuleto

Brown
Estate

Rt 121

Rt 121

Oakville

Chappellet

Nichelini

Silverado Trail

Yountville

# Southern Napa Hotels & Restaurants

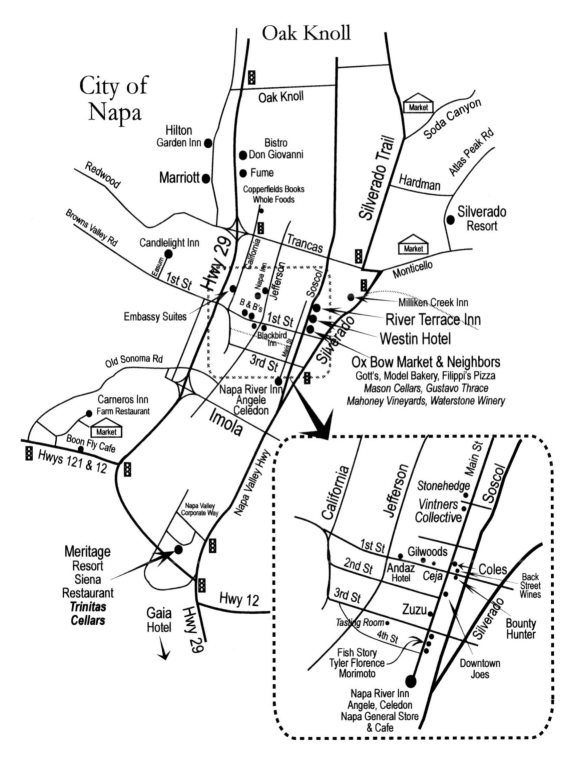

Oak Knoll

City of Napa

Oak Knoll

Market

Soda Canyon

Hilton Garden Inn

Bistro Don Giovanni

Silverado Trail

Atlas Peak Rd

Redwood

Fume

Marriott

Hardman

Copperfields Books Whole Foods

Silverado Resort

Browns Valley Rd

Candlelight Inn

Market

Trancas

California

Easum

1st St

Hwy 29

Napa Inn

Jefferson

Soscol

Monticello

Milliken Creek Inn

Embassy Suites

B & B's

1st St

River Terrace Inn

Silverado

Westin Hotel

Blackbird Inn

Main St

3rd St

Ox Bow Market & Neighbors

Old Sonoma Rd

Gott's, Model Bakery, Filippi's Pizza
*Mason Cellars, Gustavo Thrace*
*Mahoney Vineyards, Waterstone Winery*

Napa River Inn
Angele
Celedon

Imola

Carneros Inn
Farm Restaurant

Market

Boon Fly Cafe

Hwys 121 & 12

Napa Valley Hwy

Napa Valley Corporate Way

California

Jefferson

Main St

Soscol

Stonehedge

Vintners
Collective

Meritage
Resort
Siena
Restaurant
*Trinitas Cellars*

1st St

Gilwoods

2nd St

Andaz
Hotel

Ceja

Coles

Back
Street
Wines

Hwy 12

3rd St

Zuzu

Silverado

Bounty
Hunter

Gaia
Hotel

Hwy 29

Tasting Room

4th St

Fish Story
Tyler Florence
Morimoto

Downtown
Joes

Napa River Inn
Angele, Celedon
Napa General Store
& Cafe

Tours, Overviews & Maps

# Central Napa Hotels & Restaurants

## Yountville Hotels

Hwy 29
Washington St
Yountville Cross Rd
Madison
Yount St

Meadowoods
Meadwood Ln
Howell Mt Rd
Tra Vigne Pizza
Tra Vigne Restaurant
Madrone
Pope
Sunshine
Market
Gott's Roadside
Restaurant
St Helena
V Sattui deli
Dean & DeLuca
Market
Inglewood
Zinfandel
Rutherford Hill
Rutherford
Auberge Du Soleil
Rancho Caymus Inn
Rutherford Grill
Rubicon
Rutherford Cr Rd
Oakville
Silverado Trail
Robert Mondavi
Opus One
Market
Oakville Grade
Oakville Cross Rd
Mustards Grill
Brix
Yountville
Yountville Cross Rd
Domaine Chandon
Market
Poetry Inn
California
The Cottages of Napa Valley

Napa Valley Lodge
North Block
Bordeaux House
Vintage Inn
Lavender Inn
P
Maison Fleurie
Bardessono
Villagio Inn & Spa
Market
Hotel Yountville
California

## Yountville Restaurants & Tasting Rooms

Hwy 29
Washington St
Yountville Cross Rd
Madison
Girard TR
Ciccio's Restaurant
Pancha's Bar
Jessup Winery TR
Ma(i)sonry TR
Redd Wood Restaurant
Yount St
The French Laundry
P
Bouchon
Restaurant & Bakery
Bottega
Hurley's
Hill TR
Pacific Blues Cafe
Bistro Jeanty
Somerston TR
Market
Domaine Chandon Etoile Restaurant
Redd
Ad Hoc
California

# Northern Napa
## Hotels
## & Restaurants

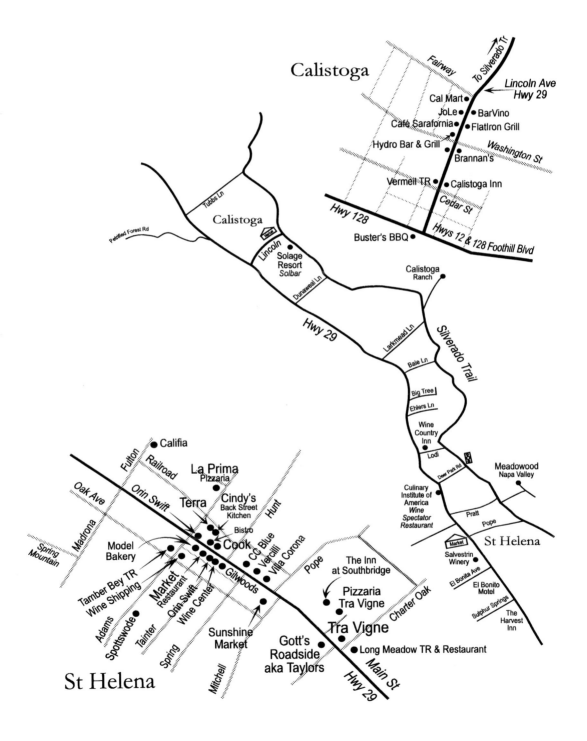

**Calistoga**

Fairway

To Silverado Tr

Lincoln Ave
Hwy 29

Cal Mart
JoLe
BarVino
Café Sarafornia
FlatIron Grill
Hydro Bar & Grill
Washington St
Brannan's
Vermeil TR
Calistoga Inn
Cedar St
Hwy 128
Hwys 12 & 128 Foothill Blvd
Buster's BBQ

Tubbs Ln

Calistoga

Petrified Forest Rd

Lincoln

Solage
Resort
Solbar

Dunaweal Ln

Hwy 29

Calistoga
Ranch

Larkmead Ln

Bale Ln

Silverado Trail

Big Tree

Ehlers Ln

Wine
Country
Inn

Lodi

Deer Park Rd

Meadowood
Napa Valley

Culinary
Institute of
America
Wine
Spectator
Restaurant

Pratt

Pope

St Helena

Califia

Fulton
Railroad

La Prima
Pizzaria

Oak Ave
Orin Swift

Cindy's
Back Street
Kitchen

Terra

Hunt

Bistro

Madrona

Spring
Mountain

Model
Bakery

Cook
CG Blue
Varcilli
Villa Corona

Market
Restaurant

Tamber Bey TR
Wine Shipping

Gilwoods

Orin Swift
Wine Center

Pope

The Inn
at Southbridge

Charter Oak

Salvestrin
Winery

El Bonita Ave
El Bonito
Motel

Sulphur Springs
The
Harvest
Inn

Adams
Spottswode
Tainter

Spring
Mitchell

Sunshine
Market

Pizzaria
Tra Vigne

Tra Vigne

Gott's
Roadside
aka Taylors

Long Meadow TR & Restaurant

Hwy 29
Main St

**St Helena**

Tours, Overviews & Maps

# For the Most Up to Date
## Information About Wine Country Use Our:

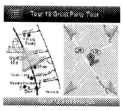

# Mobile Apps

## The Napa Valley Wine Tour
## The Sonoma Winery Tour
## for iPhone, iPad and Droid
## Through Sutro Media

Written by experienced local tour guides, *Ralph & Lahni de Amicis*, these user friendly Apps make planning and navigating fun daytrips and serious collecting adventures easy. Brief articles explain tasting room etiquette, how to extend tasting endurance and sensitivity, navigation hints, tasting fees, best routes from city to country and dress code; aka 'wine country casual'. Each winery listing includes a description, map, photo gallery, GPS Interface, contact info, wine lists, tasting fees, hours, websites, nearby wineries, navigation hints and a hospitality rating based on client feedback. Some listings include video links.

**The directories can be sorted to find** hidden gems, wineries with tours, caves, gardens, picnic tables, etc., and by region, distance and cost.

**Get the honest, inside story** on whether a winery is dynamite or a dud, which have the best wines, deals, views, tours, and picnic spots among the vines. *This is the App that the local Limo drivers and Tour Guides use* and contribute information to, yet the easy format makes it perfect for the casual day tripper and first time visitor. ***Very Reasonably Priced! Updated Frequently!***

## On the iPhone and Droid Stores from Sutro Media:
**Sonoma Winery Tour:** 200+ wineries, with 2000+ original photos, 10 mapped tours.

**Napa Valley Winery Tour:** 250+ wineries, with 2000+ original photos, 20 Mapped Tours.

# Chapter 7: Using the Directory and Maps

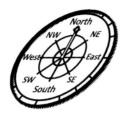

**One**: Unless you have a designated driver, don't visit more than two wineries, with lunch between, because that would be too much wine to still drive safely. Select the wineries that seem most interesting and take the time to enjoy them.

**Two**: A well-planned route makes mostly right-hand turns, the reason that we show other wineries along the way is to encourage a sense of adventure. If you take your time and drive like an adult, you will be perfectly safe, no matter how you change the order of the wineries around.

**Three**: The information pages by the maps include navigation hints. The time does not include getting into and out of the car, which, with a larger group, can be time-consuming. Among Wine Country guides managing large groups is called "herding cats", requiring both patience and a sense of humor.

**Four**: Signs. This is an agricultural area and signs are often not obvious. Many Napa wineries are allowed just two, relatively small **white on blue signs** as the sole guidepost to their entranceways. They are hard to spot at fifty miles an hour. Many other wineries are only marked by a street number. It is one of the reasons people hire guides, and even they miss the entrances now and then. Napa crossroads are marked with signs about one hundred or more feet before the actual road. There often is no sign at the road itself, or it may be across from the road on a foliage obscured pole. This is an aspect of agricultural roads that city and suburban dwellers may find odd. When you see the sign warning of the road ahead, start slowing down and watch the painted lines on the asphalt as your indicators. They will tell you where to turn. This is especially helpful when the grass is high, or the vines are filled with leaves and encroaching on the edges of the roads. Late in the season the road paint often wears thin and the bushes lean into the roads so pay attention! Sonoma has large white sign posts pointing towards the wineries and fewer restrictions on additional signs.

**Five**: If you want to visit the full gamut of wineries and not have to spit out the wine, then hire a driver, or better yet, a qualified driver/tour guide. If the driver knows the area well, great! If they do not know the area, the map section is filled with well-tested tours. If the driver you hire is concerned about the practicality of the tours, tell them this: Many of these tours were developed while driving big SUVs, stretched limousines and small buses. If drivers can fit a thirty-foot limousine along these routes safely, you should have no problem driving a convertible Mustang.

## Our Winery Picks & Tasting Fees

We choose wineries that are easy to drop by, or visit by making an easy appointment. So, we left out 100's of very small wineries where it is a lot of work to make an appointment, unless you are a tour guide bringing sure fire buyers. We selected wineries for the mapped tours because of their great hospitality, the beauty of their locations and the quality of their wines. A good tour is like a good meal, made up of complementary components that fit together nicely. But wineries get better and worse in their hospitality just like their wines so we've created a rating system based on measurable factors that we post in our Smart Phone Applications. To get our current suggestions, buy our Apps which are listed at the back of the book.

## Key to the Tasting Fees

Wineries have a range of fees from modest for their less expensive wines, to expensive for their reserve and library tastings and tours. The nice thing about a tasting fee is that it frees you from feeling obligated to buy a wine that you don't want, for whatever reason. Some wineries waive all, or part of the tasting fee, based on how much wine you purchase.

$ Free to Modest, $0-$5. $$ Average, $10-$15.
$$$ Serious, $20-$30. $$$$ Very Serious, over $35-$50. $$$$$ Pricey, usually including a tour & food pairing or seminar, over $50 and up. $ - $$$ The dollar signs separated by a dash represents a range of prices.

**CWP** – **C**omplimentary **W**ith **P**urchase,
**PIE** – **P**urchase **I**s **E**xpected, at very small wineries in lieu of a tasting fee. This **PIE** designation is our opinion, not the policy of the wineries.

***Appointment*** Instant - Regulations require an appointment, but they are often open to you dropping in and setting up the appointment right then and there, if scheduling permits.

**TF** - Tasting Fee,  **Hrs** - Hours,  **TR** - Tasting Room, as compared to a winery site.

**Wine Name Abbreviations**: Cabernet Sauvignon/Franc - Cab Sauv/Franc Chardonnay - Chard  Sauvignon Blanc - Sauv Blanc  Zinfandel - Zin

# Chapter 8: Directory of Napa Wineries

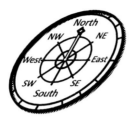

**Acacia Winery** - Carneros with Views - Wines: Pinot Noir, Chard - 2750 Los Amigas Rd. Napa CA 94559 - www.acaciawinery.com - (707) 226-9991 - TF: $$ - Hrs: 10-4 by Appt.

One of the nice things about Acacia is that it is so convenient, just a couple of minutes off of Route 121 behind Domaine Carneros. It sits in the rolling hills of Los Carneros, which is the only area of Napa where the vines run over the hills like a carpet. Being just north of the Bay this area is always cooler than the northern valley, so in the midst of the hot summer this is a great place to taste. They are by appointment, but the staff is very relaxed, and the tasting room is spacious, so as you are driving there, call them on the phone and make an instant appointment. If you forget to, go inside and see if they are busy. This side of Carneros is rarely busy.

There are nice tables outside, although they are not permitted for picnics. This is a large winery so it is hard to miss, and the tasting room is tucked up against the equipment, so you can smell the wine process through the doorways. They have wide distribution and make the crisp clean flavors that Carneros wines are known for, sourcing their grapes from within sight of the winery. **MAP 15**

**A Dozen Vintners** - Collective Tasting Room at Lodi Lane - 3000 St. Helena Hwy Hwy 29 at Lodi Lane - www.adozenvintners.com - (707) 967-0666 - TF: $$ - Hrs: 10-5

This is a collective tasting room on Route 29 at the corner of Lodi lane. Probably the nicest part of the experience is that they are located up valley. Normally tasting rooms are found downtown, and this one is just minutes from a number of nice wineries, and across the way from the Culinary Institute of America at Greystone. **MAP 10**

**Aetna Springs Cellars** - Small Pope Valley Winery - Wines: Cab Sauv, Cab Franc, Syrah - 7227 Pope Valley Rd. Pope Valley CA 94567 - www.aetnaspringscellars.com (707) 965-2675 - TF: PIE - Hrs: Appt

The Pope Valley parallels the Napa Valley to the northeast. It is a bit of a ride to Aetna Springs Cellars, which is a very small winery producing about 500 cases per year. The grapes are sourced from ten acres there. The winery is under the owner's house tucked into the hillside. Be aware that Pope Valley is hotter than the Napa Valley and all of the roads to get there are winding and fairly steep, since it is on the other side of the mountains in the next easterly valley. However, the drive is beautiful and, if you are adventurous, then make the trip. Make an appointment, because that way you'll be assured that they will see you. This is a winery for the serious, although the prices are very good as is the quality of the wines. **MAP 13**

**Allora Vineyards** - Very Small Family Winery by Appointment - Wines: Cab Sauv, Petite Sirah - 3244 Ehlers Ln. St. Helena CA 94574 - www.alloravineyards.com - (707) 963-6071 - TF: PIE - Hrs: by Appt

This is a very small winery where the barrel room and very comfortable tasting room are below the beautiful house. While there is a barrel cave, there is no winery on the site. The owners are builders and the place is beautiful and the tasting is normally done by the family. These are some wonderful wines that will appeal to serious enthusiasts, but their production is about 1000 cases so they sell out quickly. They also sell some great wine glasses of their own design. Wines: Cabernet Sauvignon, Petite Sirah. **MAP 11**

**Alpha Omega** - Fun, delicious experience - Wines: Bordeaux & Burgundy - 1155 Mee Ln. St. Helena CA 94574 - www.aowinery.com - (707) 963-9999 - TF: $$$ - CWP - Hrs: 10-6

This is an up and coming winery, on a side street just off of Route 29. They can be seen from Route 29. The winery has been under construction with one improvement after the other, and it shows. From the road, you can see the fountains soaring into the sky. When you sit outside on the tasting patio, you find yourself enjoying the cooling spray, now and then, if the wind comes from the correct quarter.

They make wonderful wines, with a fantastic staff and the place is a lot of fun. This is especially popular with a younger crowd. They have both a tasting bar and sit down tastings outside on the patio. Their patio is a nice place for a picnic. **Map 18**

**Altamura Winery** - Premium and Private - Wines: Cab Sauv , Sangiovese - 1700 Wooden Valley Rd. Napa  CA  94558 - www.altamura.com – (707) 253-2000 -  TF: PIE  - Hrs: by Appt

They are a premium wine maker with long ties to the Valley and a great reputation, producing about 5000 cases yearly. Their 400 acre property is located nine miles east from downtown Napa in an area with no other wineries. They have just finished a new winery building, which is tucked off the road. There are plans to put a tasting room on Wooden Valley Road. The wines are wonderful, not cheap and appointments require lots of advance notice. Wines: Cabernet Sauvignon, Sangiovese. **MAP 6**

**Amizetta Vineyard** - A Long Drive - Wines: Cab Sauv & Blends - 1099 Greenfield Rd. St Helena CA 94574 - www.amizetta.com - (707) 963-1460 - TF: $ - Hrs: 10-4 by Appt

They are 6.1 miles from Silverado Trail at the eastern edge of the Napa Valley. This is a small family winery, very much by appointment. In fact, when you make the appointment they give you a gate code because there is no call box at the gate. The winery sits at about 1000 feet elevation with great views of Lake Hennessey. They produce very high quality wines, and their winery and cave hosts several other small producers. **MAP 13**

**Ancien Wines** - Small by Appointment - Wines: Burgundy - East Napa, Ca 94581 - www.Ancienwines.com - (707) 927-6594 - TF: PIE - Hrs: By Appt Call for directions. **MAP 6**

**Anderson's Conn Valley Vineyards** – Caves in the Eastern Hills - Wines: Cab Sauv, Pinot Noir, Chard - 680 Rossi Rd. St. Helena CA 94574 - www. connvalleyvineyards.com -
(707) 963-8600 - TF: PIE - Hrs: Appt

Conn Valley is 10-15 minutes from the Silverado Trail, up narrow winding roads, through low rolling hills and to beautiful, rustic wineries. This is also the family's home and the site of two wineries. The tasting usually includes a tour of the caves and the owners often lead the tour. It is a beautiful location off the beaten track. The wines are very good and the experience is relaxed, friendly and informative. In the winter, they do the tasting in the house. This is also the site of the Eagle's Trace label. **MAP 13**

**Andretti Winery** - Oak Knoll Italian Style - Wines: Chard, Merlot, Cab Sauv, Sauv Blanc, Pinot Grigio, Pinot Noir, Sangiovese, Zin-Primitivo Blend. 4162 Big Ranch Rd. Napa CA 94558  www.andrettiwinery.com  (707) 259-6777  TF: $$ - $$$  Hrs: 10-5

Oak Knoll is just north of the city of Napa and filled with many great, family run wineries. This is a 'must visit' for racing buffs, being Mario Andretti's winery. It has an Italian-style, even though the section of Italy where their family comes from originally, close to Trieste, is no longer part of Italy. They have nice gardens, cute gifts, tours, and tables.

Be aware that its very convenient location and brand name means that it is a popular stop for tour and wine shuttle buses. However, just because there is a bus parked there doesn't mean they are in the tasting room, so walk inside and check it out. It is a lot nicer in the summer than in the winter, something about those Tuscan style buildings that feel a little drafty in the cool and wet. But, generally, this is a very nice experience, good, value wines and very convenient just minutes from downtown Napa. Tours by appointment. **MAP 5**

**Arger-Martucci Vineyards** - Small but Convenient - Wines: Chard, Viognier, Rosé. Pinot Noir, Syrah, Cab Sauv. 1455 Inglewood Ave. St. Helena CA 94574 www.arger-martucciwine.com (707) 963-4334 TF: $$$ Hrs: 10-4

This small winery was formed by a partnership of two families, doing about 5000 cases per year. When you pull in you see the winery in front of you. The tasting room is in the kitchen of the old guest house, although many of the tastings are done outside around the pool. You can bring a picnic to enjoy with your tasting. They are by appointment, but on a quiet day try dropping by, because sometimes it is hard to get them on the phone. Be aware that they are a popular stop for small tour buses that take over a table or two, so if you get there and the tables are packed; remember that there are other good wineries nearby. **Map 18**

**Artesa Winery** - Spectacular View in Southern Napa Carneros - Wines: Burgundy, Bordeaux and Spanish. 1345 Henry Rd. Napa 94559 www.artesawinery.com (707) 224-1668 Hrs: 10-5 TF: $$ - $$$

This is a great destination winery with spectacular views of Carneros and the Bay. It was built by a great Spanish winery that removed the top of the hill, built the winery and replaced the top with the winery inside at a cost of 30 million dollars. It has stunning architecture, incredible glass sculptures and fountains to die for. The spacious tasting room becomes a fun bar scene on the weekends, and there is plenty of room to spread out. Take the tour of the caves and winery beneath your feet because it's worth seeing. Don't miss strolling on the side patios with a glass of wine in your hand, where you can see the DeRosa Art Preserve down below, and Domaine Carneros Winery, owned by the French Champagne family Taittinger. Sit out there late in the day with your darling and a glass of wine and if that doesn't make you feel romantic, you're just not doing it right. Wines: Cabernet Sauvignon, Chardonnay, Merlot, Pinot Noir, Tempranillo, Albariño, Blends. Just across Hwy 12 are wineries Domaine Carneros, Cuvaison, Bouchaine and by appointment Adastra. **MAP 15**

**Atalon Winery** - Premium Producer - Wines: Sauv Blanc, Merlot, Cab Sauv. 3299 Bennett Ln. Calistoga CA 94515 www.atalon.com (800) 224-4090 (707) 9423602 TF: $$ Hrs: 10-4 by Appt

This is a high end producer who has high quality grape sources and a beautiful, although remote location. Located north of downtown Calistoga they are a long ride from San Francisco, but if you are staying in either Napa or Sonoma this is a great place to visit, assuming you like big reds with a great pedigree. The wines are expensive, even though this is newer winery. The wines were previously tasted at Cardinale. Both are owned by Jess Jackson, of Kendall Jackson fame. **MAP 10**

**August Briggs Wines** - Downtown TR - Wines: Pinot Meunier, Zin, Pinot Noir, Chard, Syrah, Petite Sirah, Cab Sauv. 1307 Lincoln Ave.   Calistoga  CA 94515      www.augustbriggswines.com   (707) 942-4912   TF: $   Hrs: 11 - 5

August Briggs is a family-owned winery located in dontown Calistoga. They produce limited quantities of wines sourced from vineyards in the North Coast counties. Taste in their small, interestingly designed and very social tasting room. **MAP 10**

**Baldacci Vineyards** - Stags Leap District Family Winery - Wines: Cab Sauv, Pinot Noir.  6236 Silverado Trail   Napa  CA  94558 www.baldaccivineyards.com  (707) 944-9261   TF: $  CWP   Hrs: 10-5 by Appt

This is one of the 22 wineries in the Stags Leap district at the south eastern corner of the Napa Valley. This is a wonderful, small family-run winery tucked into a southern facing hillside, surrounded by some of Napa's most famous labels. They have great caves, a charming tasting room and a very loyal wine club and clientele. They do wonderful events, mostly in the caves, and the tasting room/building has some interesting features. If you see any redheads, that's probably a member of the family. From here, you can easily visit the Silverado Vineyards, Pine Ridge, Robert Sinskey and of course Stag's Leap. These are great folks with wonderful connections in the area. Wines: Cabernet Sauvignon, Pinot Noir. They are by appointment and being small, and wanting to do a good job for their guests, they really like it when you call ahead. However, the drive is usually open, so call them at the last minute and see if they are pouring. **MAP 6**

**Ballentine Vineyards Wines** - Wide Variety of Wines - Wines: Cab Sauv, Chenin Blanc, Zin, Merlot, Cab Franc, Syrah, Petite Sirah, Petit Verdot.  2820 St Helena Hwy N. St. Helena  CA  94574   www.ballentinevineyards.com (707) 963-7919   TF: $  CWP
Hrs: 10-5 by Appt instant

This is a very small winery in a great location, although it looks more like a warehouse than a chateau in France, or even a California ranch house. It sits right across the street from St. Clement and next to Markham. The wines are from their own grapes, the tasting room is being redone, and the tasting is very relaxed. The wines are good and great value. The Ballentine family has a long history in the valley. The sign is only visible as you are traveling north. When you are heading south, remember they are right across the road from St. Clement. **MAP 10**

**Barnett Vineyards** - Spring Mountain Views - Wines: Cab Sauv, Pinot Noir, Chard.  4070 Spring Mountain Rd.  St. Helena  CA  94574  www.barnettvineyards.com   (707) 963-7075   TF: $$$$  Hrs: 10-4 by Appt

This is a charming small winery, with a great reputation, clinging to the side of Spring Mountain, producing spectacular wines. There is almost no flat land on their site. They enjoy incredible views of the valley below, which you get to enjoy since the tasting is outside on patios built into the hillside. They have an excellent staff, it is a great place for a picnic, but make your appointment early so you don't miss out. The tasting starts in the winery/barrel room. Go on a tour of the vineyard if you can, they are all hillside grown grapes, and many people believe those are the best. That's because grapes do not like wet feet, so hillsides provide excellent drainage. They are nearby Pride Mountain Winery, Schweiger and Terra Valentine, which are all also by appointment. Remember to bring a lunch from downtown St. Helena (the Sunshine Market or Dean and DeLuca are good places to pick up a sandwich) because there are no stores on the mountain. **MAP 12**

**Beau Vigne** - Tasting room - Wines: Cab Sauv, Chard.  6795 Washington St Yountville, CA 94599 www.BeauVigne.com (707) 947-7058 TF: $$$$ Hrs: 10 (11) -6 (7) Seasonal,

**Beaulieu Vineyard** - Grand Old Winery - Wines: Cab Sauv, Chard, Pinot Noir, Merlot, Zin, Syrah, Sauv Blanc, Shiraz, Sangiovese, Viognier, Port, Blends.  1960 St Helena Hwy (Hwy 29).  Rutherford  94559  www.bvwines. com  (707) 967-5230  TF: $ - $$$  Hrs: 10-5

This is one of Napa's grand old wineries that survived Prohibition by getting a license to make church wines. The name means Beautiful View, although a hundred years later it's surrounded by buildings, but its central location and great value wines keeps it a winner. Their basic Napa Valley Cabernet Sauvignon is a steal at $30. Their main tasting room is spacious and offers a wide line of wines. The extensive gift shop is downstairs.

Across the way is the pricier Reserve room, with white marble counters and racks holding generations of revered vintages. This is where they pour their best, BIG RED wines. The reserve room staff may be a little stodgy, but it's a wonderful setting and they pour great wines. It's a good idea to share that tasting because the alcohol levels are pretty hot, if you know what we mean. Their revered Russian winemaker and vineyard manager, Andre Tchelistcheff (now passed), was trained in France. He was the source of many major winemaking innovations used internationally today, and he acted as a guide and mentor to many of the areas most important growers and winemakers. There is a statue of him outside the reserve room. Beaulieu is commonly known by its initials 'BV'. **Map 18**

**Bell Wine Cellars** - Excellent Wines by Appointment - Wines: Cab Sauv, Syrah, Port, Chard, Zin, Viognier, Merlot, Sauv Blanc. 6200 Washington Street Yountville CA 94599  www.bellwine.com  (707) 944-1673  TF: $$$ - $$$$$  Hrs: 10:30-4 by Appt

This is a small, very classy winery south of Yountville. The wines are excellent; the tasting experience is friendly & knowledgeable with multiple programs, food-pairings & reserve tastings available. The tour includes the vineyards and winery. They are by appointment and they mean it. There is no sense in dropping in and seeing if they will pour for you because they do not have that big of a staff. They have a very loyal clientele so much of their wine is shipped directly to their customers. The grounds are nice although mostly intended for the use of the wine club during events. **Map 17**

**Benessere** - A Romantic Northern Jewel - Wines: Pinot Grigio, Sangiovese, Syrah, Zin, Pinot Noir, Muscat di Canelli, Super Tuscan style blend. 1010 Big Tree Rd. St. Helena CA 94574    www.benesserevineyards.com  (707) 963-5853   TF: $$   Hrs: 10-5

This is a romantic jewel, a small, family owned winery, owned by people who have a love of all things Italian. The name means 'Well Being' in Italian and between the beautiful location, the intimate, but friendly tasting room and the wonderfully made wines that describes the place quite well. There are very few wineries in the North Bay wine country that specialize in Italian style wines. Originally, Luna aimed in that direction but now they only make a popular Pinot Grigio, which they don't even serve at the winery most days. Over in Sonoma there are several wineries with the Italian spirit; Seghesio in Healdsburg, and then Jacuzzi and Viansa in Sonoma Carneros. Benessere does a good job with the Italian varietals and they make a nice change to the barrage of Cabernet Sauvignon and Chardonnay that the valley seems awash in. There are tables outside under the rose arbor in case you want to have a snack. There are also Sangiovese vines by the front door. **MAP 11**

**Bennett Lane Winery** - Worth the Ride - Navigation Tip: Their driveway is located on Hwy 128. Bennett Lane is south of the winery. Wines: Chard, Cab Sauv, Blends. 3340 Highway 128 Calistoga CA 94515    www.bennettlane. com (707) 942-6684   TF: $$   Hrs: 10-5:30

They are at the far northern part of the Napa Valley and so they have worked even harder to make their tasting experience attractive, with considerable success. Besides good wines, they also have picnic tables, good views, tours, and they are big on race cars, since the owners own a team. Their signature wine is called Maximus after the 2nd century Roman Emperor Magnus Maximus. They have a collection of ancient coins and each wine has a Roman coin image on the label. Several coins dating from that era are displayed. They have a great staff and they make interesting wines. On Saturdays, they pair their Maximus wines with chocolate. This was formerly the Vigil Vineyard Winery. Navigation Tip: Their driveway is located on Hwy 128. Bennett Lane is south of the winery. **MAP 10**

**Beringer Vineyards** - Great, Varied Tours - Wines: Wide variety from commercial to pricey. 2000 Main St.  St. Helena  94574    www.beringer.com

(707) 967-4412    TF: $$ - $$$    Hrs: 10-6 (10-5 winter)

Beringer, just north of downtown St Helena, is one of the most visited wineries, but it's so spread out that it rarely feels crowded. Continuously in operation since in 1876, today the mansion and old winery building house the tasting rooms and gift shops. The modern winery is across the street. Owned by the Foster's Beer Company, who understands hospitality, they offer a wide variety of wines and tours. The most charming tasting experience is of the reserve wines in the gorgeous Beringer Mansion which was patterned after the family home in Germany. The walk-in tasting is excellent. They also do sit down tastings by appointment upstairs where they roll out the 'best'.

Many of these Mansion wines are sold only at the winery, so if you have an impression of Beringer as 'white Zinfandel', be prepared to have that idea knocked out of the park. The grounds are great for strolling, and to the left of the Mansion are rarely noticed, shaded picnic tables. Pick up a picnic at Dean and DeLuca or the Sunshine Market in St Helena and enjoy. Wines: Chardonnay, Dessert Wines, Sauvignon Blanc, Pinot Noir, Merlot, Cabernet Sauvignon, Riesling, Viognier, White Zinfandel, White Merlot, Chenin Blanc, Pinot Grigio, Syrah. Just north is the Culinary Institute of America at Greystone, a great non-wine stop and St Clement winery and Markham, and by appointment Joseph Phelps. **MAP 10**

**Black Stallion Winery** - Southern Silverado Trail - Wines: Chard, Pinot Grigio, Sauv Blanc, Muscat Canelli, Rose', Merlot, Syrah, Cab Sauv. 4089 Silverado Trail   Napa CA 94558    www.blackstallionwinery.com (707) 253-1400    TF: $ - $$$$   Hrs: 10-5

This is a newer winery opened in a completely transformed stone building that was once an equestrian center. They are very conveniently located on the southern edge of the Silverado Trail just minutes north of downtown Napa. They have a spacious, beautifully appointed tasting room, including wonderful seating areas for special tastings and a very comfy room just for the wine club. To the side they have a spacious outdoor tasting area complete with bar, although you sit shaded, at tables under fans, for the hot weather. Their high end red blend is named Bucephalus, after the horse of Alexander the Great. The tasting bar is large, which is good since they get very busy at the end of the day. They have very easy parking. The wines are coming along. They are nearby the Reynolds Family winery, Darioush and Luna. Navigation Tip: Enter by the driveway directly in front of the winery. It is more dramatic. The drive will bring around back to the entrance way.   **Map 17**

**Bouchaine Vineyards**  - Carneros Views - Wines: Chard, Pinot Noir, Pinot Gris, Syrah, Pinot Meunier, Gewürztraminer. 1075 Buchli Station Rd.  Napa CA  94559  www.bouchaine.com  (707) 252-9065  TF: $$$  Hrs: 10:30 - 5

This is one of the jewels of Los Carneros, in the southern edge of the

County, just north of the bay. They enjoy the Carneros winds that keep the area cool and perfect for Pinot Noir and Chardonnay, which they do quite well. Their outdoor seating area is a great place to bring a picnic and, if you are filling your wine cellar, this is a great value. They have a wonderfully friendly staff and a pretty lawn and tasting room if it is too cool or hot outside. The preferred for the tasting is outside on the patio. The tastings are very reasonable, although you should visit in the early part of the day, first because your taste buds will be fresh, and second because they close early. This is a favorite stop for organized bike tours, but they are rarely disruptive. **MAP 15**

**Bravante Vineyards** - Howell Mountain Appointment - Wines: Bordeaux. 300 Stone Ridge Rd. Angwin CA. www.BravanteVineyards.com (707) 965-2552 TF: $$$ Hrs: By Appt **MAP 13**

**Bremer Family Winery** - Deer Park by Appointment - Wines: Cab Sauv, Merlot, Zin, Cab Franc, Claret, Petite Sirah, Port, White Port. 975 Deer Park Rd. St. Helena CA 94574 www.bremerfamilywinery.com (707) 963-5411 TF: $ Hrs: 10-5 by Appt

They are tucked up on the hillside of Howell Mountain quite far north in the Valley. The ride up Deer Park Road affords some spectacular views. The tastings are mostly outdoors in the nice weather as their tasting room is quite small. They are in process of building an extensive aging cave. The staff is very knowledgeable and relaxed and the location is great. They make very good wines and have quite a loyal customer base. **MAP 13**

**Buehler Vineyards** - Conn Valley by Appointment - Wines: Cab Sauv, Chard, Zin, White Zin. 820 Greenfield Road., St. Helena CA 94574 www. buehlervineyards.com (707) 963-2155 TF: PIE Hrs: 10-4 M-F by Appt

Founded 1978, it is 20 minutes from the Silverado Trail to reach this isolated winery, but they make some seriously good wines, yet their wines are reasonably priced. The tour is conducted by a family member and the whole experience is informative and relaxed. If you want something off the beaten path and you need to stock your cellar this is the place for you. **MAP 13**

**Burgess Cellars** - Deer Park by Appointment - Wines: Cab Sauv, Merlot, Syrah. 1108 Deer Park Rd. St. Helena CA 94574 www.burgesscellars.com (707) 963-4766 TF: PIE Hrs: 10-4 by Appt.

This land on the hillsides of Howell Mountain was first planted in the 1880's. Burgess started in 1972 when there were less than 30 wineries in Napa. They have had the same winemaker since then. Their tasting is in the barrel room, and every year they release a library wine that is at least 10 years old. This is a great experience since it gives you a chance to see how the wines mature. Grapes like Cabernet Sauvignon dramatically improve with time as the tannins soften and the flavors integrate. They have great views. **MAP 13**

**Cade Winery** - Beautiful Howell Mountain - Wines: Cab blend, Sauv Blanc/Semillon.  360 Howell Mountain Rd. S.  Angwin  CA  94508    www.cadewinery.com   (707) 945-1220    TF: $$    Hrs: By Appt

This is a state of the art winery perched on the mountains with spectacular views of the Napa Valley and great caves . It is owned by the Plumpjack Company, the same folks that own the Plumpjack winery and the Carneros Inn. It was built with a high amount of attention given to its 'green' nature, and it fits into the surroundings like a jewel crowning the mountains. They are by appointment, but they share the Plumpjack gracious sense of hospitality, so it is worth planning for. They do tours, because after all, with so much work you want to show off a bit, don't you? **MAP 13**

**Cain Vineyard & Winery** - Long Ride, Narrow Road - Wines: Bordeauz. 3800 Langtry Rd.  St. Helena  CA  94574  www.cainfive.com    (707) 963-1616   TF: $$$   Hrs: by Appt - They Charge Your Card @ Reservation time.

To reach them first you drive half way up Spring Mountain Road, and then turn left on Langtry. While it is not that steep, it certainly is narrow and winding. They are only open to appointments 2 days a week, but they have great views, a pretty building and wonderful wines, so it is worth the trouble if you have the interest. Because the appointments are in the mornings, the best strategy is to plan on heading back down the mountain for the rest of the day. Since the rest of the Spring Mountain wineries are by appointment you can't fill the time in between appointments with a walk-in winery. While appointments supposedly take a certain amount of time, good companions and wine sales can toss a schedule out the window. Then you find yourself late for the next appointment. On the valley floor, this might not pose such a problem, but up on Spring Mountain, the small size of the wineries doesn't leave much wiggle room for adjusting appointments. **MAP 12**

**Cakebread Cellars** - Popular Appointment Winery - Wines: Sauv Blanc, Chard, Pinot Noir, Merlot, Syrah, Zin, Cab Sauv, Rubaiyat (blend of Pinot Noir, Syrah & Zin).  8300 St Helena Hwy (Hwy 29).  Rutherford  CA  94573  www.cakebread.com  (800) 588-0298
TF: $$ - $$$   Hrs: 10-4 by Appt

This is one of the top ten restaurant wines for high end eateries, so when patrons visit, they want to go to Cakebread. Also, the family name Cakebread, is easy to remember. The sales/welcome space is an airy, wood lined tank room. That is where you start the tasting with Sauvignon Blanc, with the stainless steel tanks hovering over your shoulders, and the Sauv Blanc vines across the parking lot from where you are standing. They're famous for their Chardonnay, but like every Rutherford winery, their greatest pride is their Cabernet Sauvignon. They do a sit down tasting in the garden, and a brief tour, a thoroughly social, delicious experience.

The only hitch is they're by appointment and popular. You enter as part of a group, so arrive 10 minutes early, or lose your spot. Tastings take 45 minutes & tours 90, and their Chardonnay smells just like their winery. Navigation Tip: Finding the driveway is tricky because the sign isn't visible from the road. Going north on Rt 29 they are just past Turnbull. Watch for the black mailbox which has their name in white block letters. Just north are Sawyer, St. Supéry and Peju Province. Just south are Turnbull, Sequoia Grove by appointment Nickel & Nickel and Opus One. **MAP 19 & MAP 7**

**Calafia Cellars** - Very Small - Wines: Bordeaux blends. 629 Fulton Ln. St. Helena CA 94574 www.calafiacellars.com (707) 963-0114 TF: $ Hrs: by Appt Closed Jan

The owner/winemaker has some serious winemaking chops, having honed his skills at Souverain, Mayacamus, Stag's Leap Vineyard as well as Hess Collection. With a case production of only 595 cases, they make a Red Table Wine in the classic Bordeaux style. **MAP 23**

**Caldwell Vineyards** - Winery Caves - Wines: Cab Sauv, Merlot. 169 Kreuzer Ln Napa CA 94559 www.caldwellvineyard.com (707) 255-1294 TF: $$$$ Hrs: By Appt

Located to the east of the city of Napa in the beautiful hills north of the Bay. This is a place for the serious enthusiast, and in fact, the entire winery is inside a cave. The caves are dug into a steep hillside with great views of the city of Napa in the distance. The ride down to the cave is on a steep gravel drive cut into the hillside. It is a little nervous-making the first time you visit. You pass the extensive vineyards on the way in and only later realize that they are planted above the caves. The Caldwell wines are very good, elegant and interesting. The tasting experience often includes foods pairings, although being a small winery they change things up now and then, and the tasting is expensive if you are not there to buy. When they started digging the caves they got a little carried away. They are over thirty thousand square feet, and they now are home to a large collection of small winemakers who share the space and equipment. They employ some wonderful technology so the tour is fascinating for anyone with a bit of knowledge about the art of winemaking. They create a great tasting experience in a dome-shaped room carved from the native stone of the caves. Remember, the whole experience is inside the caves. For some reason this part of the valley includes a number of wineries that are entirely cave based. We've been told that it does save on real estate taxes. **MAP 6**

**Cardinale Estate Wines** - Wonderful Experience by Appointment - Wines: Cab Sauv blends. 7600 St Helena Hwy (Hwy 29). Oakville CA 94562 www.cardinale.com (707) 948-2643 TF: $$$$$ Hrs: 10:30-5 by Appt

This long, rambling stone building sits on a low hill on the east side of the road north of Yountville and directly across from Far Niente. They do an expensive tasting and it is clearly for the enthusiast. The appointments are set up at certain times, and take place in beautiful conference rooms. They have some wonderful wine educators and do some great food pairings. They make great red wines with an exclusive feel. This is the old Pepi winery, now owned by Jess Jackson, the owner of Kendall Jackson. **Map 18**

**Casa Nuestra Winery & Vineyards -** Very Small and Eccentric - Wines: ·French Colombard (botrytized), Chenin Blanc, Rosado, Tinto Classico, Cab Sauv, Merlot, Meritage, Cab Franc, Petite Sirah, Riesling. 3451 Silverado Trail N. St. Helena CA 94574 www.casanuestra.com (707) 963-5783 TF: $ CWP Hrs: 10-5 Mon-Sat (Closed Sun) by Appt, instant

This is a very small rustic winery with 60's and 70's memorabilia filling the intimate tasting room. The winery is down a small gravel road just north of the Duckhorn Winery on the Silverado Trail. They have picnic tables and organic estate grown fruit. They make some wines that are unusual for Napa. The staff is fun and relaxed. **MAP 10**

**Castello di Amorosa** - Northern Napa's Castle with Tours - Wines: Multiple from dry to sweet. 4045 N. St Helena Hwy (Hwy 29). Calistoga 94515 www.castellodiamorosa.com (707) 967-6272 TF: $$ - $$$ Hrs: 9-6, 9-5 Nov-Feb

People laughed when we called Napa Valley Disneyland for adults, and then this 12th century Tuscan-style castle/winery with 110 rooms, complete with dungeon, called "Castle of the Beloved" opened at a cost of 40 million dollars after 13 years of work. But with authentic techniques and materials, real stone and wrought iron, a drawbridge, ramparts, frescos and gloom, it is a popular movie set, photo background and is also available for events. You can rent the dungeon for Halloween. Now that's one party your friends won't forget! They offer guided & self-guided tours. Appointments are suggested and you can't enter without paying. The guided tour is a better deal but plan on 2 hours. Castles are cold in winter and cool in the summer, so dress accordingly. Children are restricted to certain tours and there are way too many stairs for babies and strollers. It's surrounded by vines, olive trees, chickens and the occasional sheep. You pay more for the experience than the wine, but the experience is pretty neat. Drive up and see the outside even if you don't plan to go in. It is a sight to be seen. **MAP 10**

**Caymus Vineyards** - Famous Red - Navigation Tip: At the junction of Conn Creek, Skellenger and Rutherford Roads. Be early for your appointment. Wines: Cab Sauv, Zin, Sauv Blanc, Chard. 8700 Conn Creek Rd. Rutherford CA 94573 www.caymus.com (707) 967-3010 TF: $$$ Hrs: 10-4

They are a premium winemaker with a great reputation; a favorite at restaurants. They do a sit down tasting for a group at specific times by appointment. Make sure you arrive 10 to 15 minutes early because they can turn you away if you are late. They are not snobbish; they just won't interrupt other people's tasting experience for the tardy. Wines: Cabernet Sauvignon, Zinfandel, Sauvignon Blanc, Chardonnay. Navigation Tip: At the junction of Conn Creek, Skellenger and Rutherford Roads. Near Frog's Leap, Rutherford Hill, Mumm, and Conn Creek. **Map 18**

**Ceja** - Downtown Napa - Wines: Chard, Sauv Blanc, Merlot, Pinot Noir, Cab Sauv, Syrah, Blends. The Tasting Room at 1248 1st St Napa CA is moving so check their site or our app  Ceja Vineyards - 1016 Las Amigas Rd. Napa CA 94559   www.cejavineyards.com  (707) 255-3954   TF: $$$   Hrs: by Appt
This is a wonderful family winery in Carneros, gracious and talented. The family first arrived in the area as migrant laborers. The next generation, college-educated and well-trained makes wonderful wines. The Carneros tasting room is totally enjoyable, a beautiful, rambling hacienda with a big kitchen. They are by appointment. They have a tasting room in downtown Napa and their hours vary with the season. They are open much later on Saturday, when they periodically offer evening Salsa lessons that continue as a dance party. They feature the paintings of local artists on their walls. **MAP 21**

**Chappellet Winery & Vineyard** - Sage Canyon by Appointment - Wines: Cab Sauv, Merlot, Cab Franc, Chard, Chenin Blanc, Cuvee.     1581 Sage Canyon Rd.  St. Helena CA 94574    www.chappellet.com (707) 963-7136   TF: $$ - $$$$    Hrs: Appt at specific times
This is a world class, family run winery on the slopes of Pritchard Hill hills off Sage Canyon east of the main valley on a beautiful property. The winery was started in 1967 when there were very few wineries in Napa, and they happen to have chosne a perfect location for growing very high end Bordeaux style wines. Their wines are well known and respected and the tasting is a great experience. They make appointments at specific times. These are mountain roads, small and winding, so get the directions and map beforehand from the winery, because there are only a few signs and those are not very helpful. The online maps are of no help. It takes some effort but it is well worth the effort. Allow at least twenty minutes from the Silverado Trail to their front door. That way you won't be late. Wines: Cabernet Sauvignon, Merlot, Cabernet Franc, Chardonnay, Chenin Blanc, Cuvee. Navigation Tip: There is no sign on Sage Canyon Road other than the number #1581. This is common with many private wineries that are only open by appointment. The numbers are the right hand side across from the boat ramp on the lake. **MAP 20**

**Charbay Winery & Distillery Wines** - Top of Spring Mountain - Wines: Chard, Cab Sauv, Petite Sirah Port Dessert Wines. 4001 Spring Mountain Rd.  St. Helena CA 94574   www.charbay.com   (707) 963-9327   TF: $$$ Hrs: 10-4 Tue-Sat by Appt . They are known for their flavored Vodkas, but unfortunately, the county only permits the wines and ports to be tasted. Their Vodkas flavors include: Blood Orange, Meyer Lemon. **MAP 12**

**Charles Krug Winery** - Great History - Wines: Cab Sauv, Merlot, Sauv Blanc, Chard, Pinot Noir, Zin, Cab Franc, Syrah.   2800 St Helena Hwy N (Hwy 29) St. Helena  CA  94574  www.charleskrug.com     (707) 967-2229  TF: $ - $$$    Hrs: 10:30-5

This is Napa's oldest, still operating winery, owned by Peter Mondavi's family. It was bought by the Mondavi family the 1940's. It was when Robert left the family business that he started his own winery. The buildings have been going through an extensive, historical renovation. The family owns some wonderful vineyards up and down the Napa Valley. Considering its location next to the Culinary Institute of America at Greystone and Beringer, it is good to see that they are finally highlighting their considerable part of Napa's history. When you see the tasting room from the outside it looks very low key, but inside it is bright and fun, gracious with a great gift shop, a pleasant staff, and well made, properly priced wines. Considering its history, they are remarkably low key and friendly, and this is well worth the visit. **MAP 18**

**Chase Cellars** - Wines: Zin, Petite Sirah - 2252 Sulphur Spring Ave.  St. Helena CA 94574    www.chasecellars.com  (707) 963-1284    TF: $$$ CWP  Hrs: 10-5 by Appt   This is a very relaxed, fun, small winery down a country road just outside St. Helena, and very easy to get to. The small tasting room has great views of the valley and the young staff is great. Their specialty wines make them an exception in Cabernet mad Napa, and that's a good thing, you don't want your taste buds getting bored. The hundred year old Zinfandel vines are adjacent to the winery. Make an appointment and go see them. You'll enjoy the experience.  **MAP 4**

**Chateau Boswell** - Great Caves - Wines: Chard, Cab Sauv.  3468 Silverado Trail N.  St. Helena  CA  94574  www.chateauboswellwinery.com  (707) 963-5472  TF: $$$   Hrs: by Appt

They are located quite far north on the Silverado trail and they are housed in a remarkable building that you can see from the road. It reminds you of a small French Chateau. Their founding winemaker was the famous Andre Tchelistcheff, who guided the layout and varietal choices for the resident vineyard. These are premium wines and a place to visit for the enthusiast so make an appointment and don't expect to be rushed. They have a gorgeous, state of the art caves that connect to the winery, and all of the crush and following winemaking is done inside. They make wonderful, very small production wines, sourcing their grapes from their own three acres and from Napa and Sonoma counties. **MAP 10**

**Chateau Montelena Winery** - Of Judgment of Paris & Bottle Shock Fame - Wines: Chard, Cab Sauv, Zin, Riesling. 1429 Tubbs Ln.  Calistoga  94515  www.montelena.com(707) 942-5105    TF: $$ - $$$$  Hrs: 9:30-4

Montelena's Chardonnay took top honors against the French in the

1976 Judgment of Paris blind tasting, helping catapult Napa to the top of the wine world. They're just outside Calistoga so it's a hike from San Francisco, but since they were featured in the movie Bottle Shock, all about that infamous competition, they've spruced the place up. It is a gorgeous, classic building from the 1800's, with remarkable grounds and a beautiful lake. The tasting room is small compared to the winery, but the staff, which tends to be young, pretty and quite knowledgeable, enjoys the well-deserved Hollywood glow, making the experience fun and memorable. They make excellent wines, and you can arrange a sit down tasting with a wine educator and the top wines where you" hear the inside stories. They also do tours. The bocce courts are fun but they are short on usable picnic tables. **MAP 10**

**Chiarello Family Vineyards** - Downtown  Inside NapaStyle store - Wines: Rose of Zin, Zin, Cab Sauv.  6525 Washington St   Yountville  CA  94599 www.chiarellovineyards.com  (707) 256-0750  TF: $$$   Hrs: 10-6  Sun 10-5

Michael Chiarello's NapaStyle store in Yountville has something for everyone, and tasting his wine there is a fun experience. The wines have tons of character and will age beautifully. He brings his chef's touch to winemaking and it shows. The tasting bar is surrounded by Michael's elegant NapaStyle store in the Vintage 1870 shopping center. This is one of the most interesting stores in Yountville, a town known for great shopping. They also have a deli inside and some tables. Outside is a spacious patio. Don't miss it!  **MAP 5**

**Chimney Rock Winery** - Stags Leap's White Building - Wines: Cab Sauv, Fumé Blanc, Rosé of Cab Franc.  5350 Silverado Trail  Napa  CA  94558 www.chimneyrock.com  (707) 257-2641   TF: $$$ - $$$$   Hrs: 10-5

They are part of the Terlato Family Wineries who also own Rutherford Hill and Alderbook in Sonoma. They always do a good job of producing high quality wines and producing a satisfying tasting room experience. This is a big winery experience, not a family operation where the winemaker is pouring for you. The staff is pleasant, informative and the tasting room is pretty. It is easy to spot from the Silverado Trail being  big white, South African Dutch-style building that sits below the towering crags of Stags Leap. The original owner lived in South Africa for many years. The name comes from the golf course that preceded the winery. Apparently, the original owner loved both wine and gold. **Map 17**

**Cliff Lede Vineyards** - Charming Stags Leap District - Wines: Sauv Blanc, Cab Sauv, Claret.   1473 Yountville Cross Rd. Yountville  CA  94599   www. CliffLedeVineyards.com  (707) 944-8642   TFs: $$ - $$$   Hrs: 10-4

This is an absolutely charming winery on the northern edge of the Stags Leap district, just minutes from downtown Yountville. The staff is nice, the wines are excellent, the gardens and patio out back are gracious and relaxing. In a separate building is an art gallery with a rotating exhibit. They have a small gift area. This is a nice place for a sit down tasting with a group on a shady part of the patio. This is the tasting room. You can see the winery in the distance nestled against the hillside. The back of the winery leads into their caves. On the hillside above the winery is their associated Bed and Breakfast, the Poetry Inn, a very high end place to stay. **Map 18**

**Clos Du Val** - Stags Leap District - Wines: Cab Sauv, Chard, Merlot, Pinot Noir.  5330 Silverado Trail  Napa CA  94558   www.closduval.com (707) 261-5200   TF: $$ - $$$ CWP for classic tasting  Hrs: 10-5

This is a very much a French-style winery, with good wines, a spacious tasting room, and good picnic spot on a hot day. It was founded in 1972 by an American businessman and a French winemaker. It is still owned by the original owners and the French flag flies beside the American in front of the winery. Their Cabernet was one of the six Cabs chosen for the Judgment of Paris competition in 1976. Their neighbor, Stag's Leap Wine Cellars won. Not surprisingly they are known for their Bordeaux blends, but locally they are respected for the their Pinot which they grow in the rolling hills of Carneros on the north side of Rt. 121, off of Old Sonoma Road. They are fun to visit during crush because the grape sorters are next to the tasting room and you see and smell the process. They have Petanque Courts, some gifts, a very nice, olive tree shaded picnic area (the rest rooms are in a separate building next to the tables), and they do tours by appointment. **Map 17**

**Clos Pegase Winery** - Great  Architecture - Wines: Chard, Sauv Blanc, Pinot Noir, Merlot, Cab Sauv.  1060 Dunaweal Ln.  Calistoga  94515  (707) 942-4981  www.clospegase.com  Hrs: 10:30-5   TF: $$ - $$$

This is a dramatic building and the tasting room is tucked in the far left corner. The eclectic art collection on the grounds and inside the winery is worthy of a small museum. The building is a Michael Graves creation, the Princeton architect known for his use of vibrant colors and dramatic shapes. When you need a break from straight wine tasting, a stroll around these grounds will give your body a chance to catch up with the alcohol. They have picnic tables next to the tasting room fountain, and while it may feel strange eating in a museum, remember it's a winery. Although the wines are good, the tasting is a bit overshadowed by the surroundings. They offer free guided tours at 11 & 2. An artist in residence has been creating paintings in the tank room in the warm season and he and his dog are often willing to chat. **MAP 10**

**Conn Creek Winery** - At the Crossroads - Wines: Cab Sauv, Cab Franc, Merlot.  8711 Silverado Trail S.  St. Helena  CA  94574  www.conncreek.com (707) 963-9100  TF: $$ - $$$$  Hrs: 10-4  Tours by Appt instant  (Winter Hrs: 11-4)

This is a pleasant winery that is often missed because they are located at a busy intersection, but they make some very good wines and have a lovely staff. When they first planted the vineyards, it was so rocky that they had to use explosives to break up some of the boulders. We're sure by now the sulfur taste is gone from the vines. They do a wine blending seminar daily where people can make a bottle to their taste. They are remarkable in that they have assembled a startling array of barrels representing most of the sections of Napa. Being able to sample them side by side is a sure way to recognize how much location shapes flavors. They have some gifts, offer some tours and are convenient to many other great wineries. **Map 18**

**Constant Diamond Mountain Vineyard** - At the Top - Wines: Cab Franc, Merlot, Cab Sauv. 2121 Diamond Mountain Rd. Calistoga CA 94515 www.constantwine.com (707) 942-0707 TF: $$$$ Hrs: By Appt

This is a premium winery located at the top the mountain. The final part of the drive is so steep that they meet you and bring you up in a four wheel drive. They enjoy spectacular views and the tasting is very special, and very expensive. **MAP 10**

**Corison Wines** - A Diamond in the Rough - Wines: Cab Sauv, Gewürztraminer. 987 St Helena Hwy (Hwy 29) St. Helena CA 94574 www.corison. com (707) 963-0826 TF: $$ - $$$$ CWP Hrs: 10-5 by Appt instant

This is a centrally located, small winery owned by the respected winemaker, Cathy Corison, who is known for her stellar Cabernets. The tasting room is the barrel room located inside of a pretty barn. The tasting bar is tiny, although the room is large, so the experience really is all about the wines. Fortunately, they are very good. The staff is knowledgeable and low key. **Map 18**

**Cosentino Winery** - Next to Mustard's Grill - Wines: Bordeaux, Burgundy, Gewürzt, Sangiovese, Dolcetto, Tempranillo, Viognier, Dessert. 7415 St Helena Hwy (Hwy 29) Yountville CA 94599 - www.cosentinowinery.com - (707) 944-1220 - TF: $$ - $$$ - Hrs: 10-5

This ivy covered winery is on the west side of the road just north of Yountville. It is a high energy tasting room next to Mustard's Grill. The wines are interesting, tasty, and properly-priced, the staff is quick and fun, and they have an interesting gift section. They attract a younger crowd, and the modern style of the place reflects that. They make a wide variety of wines. **Map 18**

**Cuvaison Estate Wines** - Wines: Pinot Noir, Cab Sauv, Chard, Merlot, Syrah, Zin, Port - 4550 Silverado Trail N. Calistoga CA 94515 www.cuvaison.com (707) 942-2468 TF: $$

The old winery is in Calistoga, but the vineyards are in Carneros. This Swiss family has owned it for many years and they recently renovated their popular tasting room on the Silverado Trail. The Carneros tasting room, across from Domaine Carneros is simple, elegant with spectacular views. The Carneros tasting room is by appointment but they are always open to a request for an instant appointment. They make great Carneros wines, crisp, clean, great with food, and they have a friendly, knowledgeable staff. **MAP 10**

**Cuvaison Estate Carneros** - Great Views - Wines: Pinot Noir, Cab Sauv, Chard, Merlot, Syrah, Zin, Port. 1221 Duhig Rd. Napa CA 94559 www. cuvaison.com (707) 942-2455 TF: $$ Hrs: 10-5 by Appt Maps 11

This is their Carneros tasting room, winery and vineyards, across from Domaine Carneros is simple, elegant with spectacular views. The Carneros tasting room is by appointment but they are always open to a request for an instant appointment. Navigation Tip: Their driveway is directly across from the entrance to Domaine Carneros and the winery experiences couldn't be more different, considering the locations. **MAP 15**

**Darioush** - A Persian Dream - Wines: Viognier, Cab Sauv, Shiraz, Chard, Merlot, Pinot Noir. 4240 Silverado Trail Napa CA 94558 www.darioush. com (707) 257-2345 TF: $$$ Hrs: 10:30-5 6 or more by Appt

Any Napa visitor from Persia must come to Darioush which is at the southern end of the Silverado Trail, south of the Silverado district. It's patterned after a Persian Palace, with an elegant tasting bar, and comfy stools.

The dark, peach colored stone was quarried in Iran, carved in Italy and assembled in Napa, on top of the caves that extend beyond the building at a cost of 30 million dollars. The owner's family is from the town of Syrah in Iran, one of the birthplaces of winemaking, and they still grow grapes there today. Darioush celebrates that tradition. The tasting fee is pricey but the wines are good and a popular premium restaurant brand. Share a tasting and browse the fabulous gift shop.

The staff is friendly and the tasting starts with Viognier, the white Rhone varietal, which is a nice change from Chardonnay or Sauvignon Blanc. Despite its formal façade, it is a family friendly place and always seems to attract the prettiest girls at the end of the day. **Map 17**

**David Arthur Vineyards** - Sage Canyon by Appointment - Wines: Sauv Blanc, Chard, Merlot, Cab Sauv. 1521 Sage Canyon Rd. St. Helena CA 94574 www.davidarthur.com (707) 963-5190 TF: $$$ Hrs: by Appt

This is a respected producer perched on a ridge with spectacular views of the Valley. It is one of the wineries tucked up in the hills of Sage Canyon. The family does the tasting, very relaxed, although by appointment, and it needs to be planned in advanced, since they are scheduled. They do a great, informative tasting. **MAP 20**

**Del Dotto Estate Winery** & Caves (Zinfandel Lane) - St Helena Caves - Wines: Cab Sauv, Cab Franc, Merlot, Pinot Noir, Sangiovese, Zin, Port. 1445 St Helena Hwy (Hwy 29) St. Helena CA 94574 www.DelDottoVineyards. com (707) 256-3332 TF: $$ - $$$$$ Hrs: 11-5 by Appt (instant)

This is their newer property by their vineyards near the intersection of Zinfandel Lane and Route 29; look for the two large amphorae outside the gates. The winery is mostly underground and remarkable in an explosion of marble kind of way. You walk downstairs when you arrive. They are by appointment but open to last minute requests. In fact the 'by appointment sign' is hiding behind one of those amphora. The tastings can be expensive but the tours into the caves are fun and educational. **Map 18**

**Del Dotto Vineyards** (Atlas Peak) - Historic Caves - Wines: Cab Sauv, Cab Franc, Merlot, Pinot Noir, Sangiovese, Zin, Port. 1055 Atlas Peak Rd. Napa CA 94558 www.DelDottoVineyards.com (707) 256-3332 TF: $$ - $$$$$ Hrs: 11-5 by Appt

Their caves on Atlas Peak Road are some of the oldest in Napa, built by the architect of Inglenook and Greystone. The Del Dotto team takes a very hands-on approach and tastings are normally done as part of a tour. They love to show how various barrels influence the flavors of the wine. Both wineries, old and new, are remarkable in their own ways. The wines are very popular, the tour is a lot of fun and they draw plenty of repeat visitors. They are known to pour big tastings, so either hire a driver, or have a designated driver. The interior is elaborate. **Map 17**

**Domaine Carneros** - Elegant Sparkling Wines in Southern Napa - Wines: Brut Cuvee, Brut Rosé, Le Reve Blanc de Blancs, Pinot Noir. Wines can be ordered by the glass. 1240 Duhig Rd. Napa 94559 www.domainecarneros. com (707) 257-0101 TF: $ - $$$, Hrs: 10 -6

This chateau towers over Carneros like a birthday cake with candles alight. You can't ignore it, and you shouldn't because it offers one of Napa's most romantic sparkling wine experiences. These elegant wines are served at the White House. The building is modeled on the Taittinger family's French chateau, with large patios & gorgeous tasting rooms. The building sits high because the winery is underneath and they offer tours into the depths that explain the sparkling wine 'methode champenoise'. Out in back is a second winery make non-sparkling Pinot Noir, which with Chardonnay are the main grapes used for Champagne. The sit-down tasting is either outside with the great views, or inside a tasting room reminiscent of Versailles. Wines are offered by the glass and flight, which should be shared. Sparkling wines are so light and fresh they often disguise the significant amount of alcohol they contain. The winery is open late, until 6 pm which makes it a nice place to end a day of tasting. **MAP 15**

**Domaine Chandon** - Wines: Elegant Sparkling & Still wines - 1 California Dr. Yountville 94599 www.domainechandon.com (707) 944-2280 TF: $ - $$$ by the glass Hrs: 10-5

This is a big winery across from downtown Yountville, with beautiful grounds, a large tasting bar, seating areas inside and out, where they offer snacks and side dishes. It also houses a world class restaurant called Etoile which means 'the Star', Napa's only winery based restaurant. Domaine Chandon was the first European owned Champagne Company to invest here in the 1970's, before Napa was a famous brand. It's paid off! The expansive grounds and extensive parking make Chandon popular with large groups, limos, buses, and families with children, so while it's a fun place to visit, it is not an intimate experience.

The winery is open to 5 pm, it's busy at the end of the day and turns into a bit of a party. Between its history, reputation, hospitality, tours and great wines they continue to be one of Napa's most visited locations. Wines: Brut, Blanc de Noirs, Rosé, Sparkling Chardonnay, Blanc de Blancs, Pinot Noir, Pinot Meunier, Chardonnay, Unoaked Pinot Noir Rosé, Unoaked Chardonnay. **MAP 19**

**Duckhorn Vineyards** - A Nice Sit Down Tasting  - Wines: Sauv Blanc, Merlot, Cab Sauv.   3027 Silverado Trail N.   St. Helena  CA  94574  www. duckhorn.com   (707) 967-2000  TF: $$$  Hrs: 10-4  by Appt

Their beautiful craftsman-style mansion at the corner of Lodi Lane and the Silverado Trail is a great landmark. This is the narrowest part of the valley, and across from the vineyards, the stone walls tower above the road. They do a wonderfully relaxed, although mildly expensive, sit down tasting, either in the sunny salon or out on the patio. The staff is nice, if somewhat stiff at times, probably because the arrangement encourages a feeling of table service, rather than that of an intimate tasting experience. They have a great collection of duck decoys and sculptures.The wines are very good, and the sight of the beautiful crystal glasses arrayed on the tables is charming. The grounds are lovely and the view over the vineyards in front of the winery makes a real statement; you are in the heart of wine country. The winery was sold in 2008 but the Duckhorn family continues to manage the place. **MAP 10**

**Dutch Henry Winery** - Northern Silverado  - Wines: Cab Sauv, Syrah, Argos, Zin, Pinot Noir, Cab Franc, Chard.  4310 Silverado Trail  Calistoga  CA  94515  www.dutchhenry.com  (707) 942-5771  TF: $$  CWP  Hrs: 10-4:30

This is a small, relaxed winery south of Calistoga tucked up against the mountains on the east side of the Silverado Trail. The name comes from an old mercury miner who lived in the area. The metal was popular in part because it was used to refine gold. It is a fun place and the men who run it embrace the old west theme.  **MAP 10**

**Ehlers Estate** - Small, Beautiful Winery  - Wines: Cab Sauv, Merlot, Sauv Blanc, Cab Franc, Zin.  3222 Ehlers Ln. St. Helena  CA  94574  www.ehlersestate.com   (707) 963-5972, TF: $$, Hrs: 10-4

This is a beautiful, small winery located in a great old stone barn, with an interesting tasting room. Just behind it, and visible through the windows, is the winery. Alongside is a large shaded garden with tables and bocce courts. They have a nice staff. The wines are Biodynamic. **MAP 10**

**Elizabeth Spencer Wines** - Tasting Room with Great Pinot - Wines: Sauv Blanc, Chard, Pinot Noir, Syrah, Cab Sauv.   1165 Rutherford Rd.   Rutherford CA 94573   www.elizabethspencerwines.com   (707) 963-6067   TF: $$ - $$$ Hrs: 10-6

They are located in the original brick Rutherford Post Office from 1872, just across the street from BV. The grapes are mostly from Sonoma, and they make excellent Pinot Noir and Chardonnay. They have a tiny tasting room with a great staff, but they have a great outdoor seating area that is very popular with groups of friends and families. There is no winery on site but this is a very popular stop. **Map 18**

**Elkhorn Peak** - Eastern Carneros Appt  - Wines: Pinot Noir.   200 Polson Road  Napa  CA  94558  www.elkhornpeakcellars.com  (707) 255-0504 TF: PIE   Hrs: by Appt.  The winery sits on a hillside below the 1,336 foot Elkhorn Peak. One of the first wineries in the Jamieson Canyon, starting in 1983. The area had previously been mostly cattle grazing. It is a cool, windy area that produces wonderful Pinot Noir. They have about 20 acres planted. It is a private, by appointment tasting with one of the owners. There are no signs other than the numbers. They are next door to the Kirkland Ranch winery.  **MAP 16**

**Elyse Winery Wines** - Wonderful Wines  - Wines: Zin, Cab Sauv, Petite Sirah, Syrah, Rhone Blends.  2100 Hoffman Ln. Napa  CA  94573  www.elysewinery.com  (707) 944-2900   TF: $$ CWP  Hrs: 10-5 by Appt instant

This is a down to earth, small winery with great wines. Their owner/winemaker is a top consulting winemaker for many other labels and he loves to make a wide variety of wines. You will find blends here that are unique. They have a knowledgeable staff and a convenient location. They are often recommended by people who know good wines. **Map 17**

**Envy Wines** – Near Calistoga Geyser - Wines: Cab Sauv, Petite Sirah, Sauv Blanc.  1170 Tubbs Ln.  Calistoga CA 94515  www.envywine.com  (707) 942-4670, TF: $$,  Hrs: 10-4:30 Appt

They are located down a curving road just off Tubbs lane to the north of downtown Calistoga, across from the Summers Winery. They are by appointment, but relaxed and friendly with good wines. It is a pretty building in a convenient location. **MAP 10**

**Etude** - Carneros Charm - Wines: Pinot Noir, Merlot, Cab Sauv, Pinot Blanc, Pinot Gris. 1250 Cuttings Wharf Rd.  Napa CA 94559  www.etudewines.com (707) 257-5300  TF: $$-$$$  Hrs: 10-4:30

Many of the wineries in Carneros are down home relaxed, but Etude is a bit more elegant. It is a large facility with interesting buildings and a European feel. They have been producing high quality Pinot Noir for many years and continue to do so. They do a bar tasting and a nice sit-down tasting of their more expensive wines by appointment. **MAP 15**

**Failla** - Great Pinot by Appointment  - Wines: Pinot Noir, Viognier, Syrah, Chard. 3530 Silverado Trail  St. Helena  CA  94574  www.faillawines.com  (707) 963-0530  TF: $$   Hrs: 10-5 by Appt

They make some of the best Pinot Noir in Napa because the grapes come from Sonoma's Coastal region. They have great caves and winery, much of which is currently outside as they finish the gallery part of their caves. They have a wonderful staff that works in a charming bungalow tasting room. It is a sit down tasting by appointment and you will be part of a small group. They are right across the street from the Rombauer entrance, which is good to know since the sign is small and on the mailbox, and not very obvious. **MAP 11**

**Far Niente** - A Great Tour by Appointment  - Wines: Cab Sauv, Chard, Dolce, Sauterne style.  1350 Acacia Dr. Oakville  CA  94558  www.farniente. com   (707) 944-2861  TF: $$$$$  Hrs: 10-4 by Appt Mon - Sat

This is an architectural jewel surrounded by wonderful grounds, ponds, fountains, cork oaks and event spaces. The tasting includes a great tour of the winery and the car collection. They make wonderful world-class wines, and do a sit-down tasting at specific times. The tour takes 1 & ½ hrs minimum. Make sure that you are early for your appointment, because they only allow a limited number of small groups each day. **Map 18**

**Farella-Park Vineyards** - Relaxed Family Winery  - Wines: Sauv Blanc, Merlot, Cab  Blanc, Blends.  2222 N. Third Ave.  Napa  CA  94558  www. farella.com  (707) 254-9489  TF: $$$ CWP   Hrs: by Appt

This charming winery sits in the hills on the beautiful east-side of Napa. The property is in its second generation and their knowledge of their vineyards shows in their wonderful wines. The tasting is very relaxed, at home Napa, and on a completely different level from the 'stand at the bar' tasting most people are accustomed to. They are by appointment, and while they are always open for a call, they are a small winery and normally the winemaker is pouring for you, so if possible, plan ahead. **MAP 6**

**Fleury Winery** - Seminar Tasting   - Wines: Bordeaux varietals.  950 Galleron Rd. Rutherford  CA  94574  www.fleurywinery.com  (707) 967-8333  TF: $$$$   Hrs: 9-5 by Appt

This winery is in continual transformation and improvement. It is a very fun, very high energy tasting room with great wines, presided over by the Fleury family who bring great charm and knowledge to the experience. They employ a wonderful, young team in both the winery and the tasting room and their willingness to experiment and excel is refreshing. They have a unique indoor seating area, suitable for groups. The winery facility sits outside, and it offers great opportunities to see the winemaking process. Navigation Tip: When you pass the Sullivan Winery, Fleury will be a little farther on the right hand side. The sign is not obvious, so look for the street number. You may see a sign next to it, but their approach seems to be pretty low key. But plenty of people find it. **Map 19**

**Flora Springs Winery** - Very Convenient  - Wines: Cab Sauv, Sangiovese, Merlot, Rosato, Chard, Pinot Grigio, Blends. 677 S. St Helena Hwy (Hwy 29). St. Helena  CA  94574  Tasting Room.

They also see guests and groups at the winery nearby by Appointment. www.florasprings.com   (866) 967-8032   TF: $$-$$$$$  Hrs: 10-5  They recently transformed their tasting room into a very modern, architecturally interesting place. It includes a reserve tasting room, a small gift shop, a wonderful outdoor seating area and a place for food pairings. The Tasting Room is on the same parking lot as the Dean & DeLuca market, so you can park once and taste in the process of picking up picnic supplies.  **Note**: Although most people only visit their tasting room, they also see clients and groups at the winery at 1978 W. Zinfandel Lane, around the corner from the tasting room, and tucked up against the hills on what is called the bench lands. It is a beautiful winery with a great, spacious tasting room. To visit the winery call  for an appointment  (707) 967.6723. **Map 18 & 19**

**Folie a Deux Winery** - Space Shared with Napa Cellars  - Wines: Blends, Zin, Cab Sauv, Sangiovese, Syrah.  7481 St Helena Hwy (Hwy 29). Oakville CA  94562  www.folieadeux.com   (707) 944-2565  TF: $  Hrs: 10-6  These are both owned by the Trinchero family, they make good, well-priced wines with a steady following. They have a nice picnic area. The buildings are small but comfortable and the staff is always nice. Their location just north of Yountville near Cosentino makes them very convenient. Their hours, open to 6, and their placement on the southbound side of the road, makes them convenient for a late in the day visit. **MAP 19**

**Fontanella Family Winery** - Mount Veeder Family Winery  - Wines: Chard, Cab Sauv and Zin.  1721 Partrick Rd. Napa  CA  94558     www.fontanellawinery.com (707) 252-1017  TF: $$  Hrs: By Appt

They just opened the winery recently and while it is a bit of a ride, it comes with great views. They are a charming younger couple with years of experience and they produce solid wines with lots of character.  **MAP 16**

**Forman Vineyards**  - Private and Ultra Premium  - Wines: Cab Blend, Chard. 1501 Big Rock Rd. St. Helena  CA  94574   www.formanvineyard.net (707) 963-3900  TF: PIE   Hrs: by Appt

Perched on a ridge at the base of Howell mountain, they are in their own canyon, down a steep road and make wonderful wines. Ric Forman was the founding winemaker at Sterling and takes a real hands-on, classical approach to his own label. Be on the lookout for signs as they are minimal. **MAP 13**

**Franciscan Estate** - A Grand Estate - Wines: Cab Sauv, Chard, Sauv Blanc, Merlot, Meritage. 1178 Galleron Rd. Rutherford 94574 www.franciscan. com (707) 967-3830 TF: $$ - $$$ Hrs: 10-5

Franciscan is a big winery in a Spanish style building with a spacious tasting room, surrounded by pretty grounds, fountains and a nice shaded side patio. Their grapes come from a variety of areas, including Oakville and they were once called Franciscan Oakville Estate. But, the winery is located in Rutherford and the Oakville label was dropped. You can also taste the wines of the prestigious Mount Veeder Winery here, which is located in the southwest corner of Napa, just north of Carneros. The Cabernet Sauvignon from Mount Veeder is rich in flavor with medium tannins. If you enjoy this Cabernet, the Hess Collection Winery is also on Mount Veeder. The spaciousness of the Franciscan tasting room, its central location, the quality of the wines and moderate price point makes Franciscan a popular place, especially for a younger crowd. They offer a vineyard tour, reserve tastings, and wonderful educational seminars. **Map 19**

**Frank Family Vineyards** - Gracious and Fun - Wines: Chard, Sparkling, Cab Sauv, Zin, Zin Port, Sangiovese. 1091 Larkmead Ln. Calistoga CA 94574 www.frankfamilyvineyards.com (707) 942-0859 TF: $$ Hrs: 10-5

The tasting is in a beautiful craftsman style mansion, with spacious rooms and surrounded by beautiful grounds. They have one of the best staffs in the Valley, well-known for their humor and style. This is the site of the historic Larkmead Winery and it just recently went through a major renovation so the more historic buildings are allowed to shine. They have a nice picnic area, and first-rate wines including a delicious sparkling wine in Gran Cru style, rich and creamy. They use that to start the tasting. Navigation Tip: They are quite far north in the valley, but they are near to some very well known wineries; Sterling, Clo Pegase, Twomey, Castello di Amorosa. **MAP 10**

**Freemark Abbey** - Great Traditions - Wines: Chard, Viognier, Merlot, Cab Sauv, Sauv Blanc, Zin, Zin Port, Petit Sirah, and Syrah. 3022 St Helena Hwy (Hwy 29) at Lodi Ln. St. Helena CA 94574 www.freemarkabbey.com (800) 963-9694 TF: $$ - $$$ Hrs: 10-5

The site first became a winery in 1886. The main building dates to 1899 and it was the Lombarda winery. They made a lot of wine that they shipped to the Italian stone masons in Barre, Vermont, the site of America's largest marble and granite quarries. It has passed through numerous owners and since 1966 has been owned by a group of families. They produce 40,000 cases a year of a wide variety of well-made wines. This is a very charming winery with a nice outdoor patio and lots of seating inside. You can stand at the tasting bar or make your comfortable in a more intimate setting. The view of the gardens from the patio is especially nice. **MAP 10**

**Frog's Leap Winery** - Remarkable Organic Winery - Wines: Merlot, Zin, Chard, Sauv Blanc, Cab Sauv, Syrah, Blends. 8815 Conn Creek Rd. Rutherford CA 94558 www.frogsleap.com (800) 959-4704 TF: $$ Hrs: 10-4, tours by Appt. Spring 2014 now appointment only, use website to save time.

This organic winery has a new, completely green hospitality center. The design of the building was remarkable and worth a visit unto itself. They make great wines, they have a wonderful tour and a lovely staff. They have been organic growers for many years and maintained their status even when the regulations were made more stringent. The signs on the street are not big, so watch the numbers and look for the BIG red barn on the north side of the road. There is a sign but it is small and on the fence. When you enter the property, the tasting room is to the right. If you have time for the tour, make an appointment. They do an especially nice one. **Map 19**

**Gargiulo Vineyards** - Oakville Charm - Wines: Bordeaux Blends - 575 Oakville Cross Rd Napa CA 94558 www.gargiulovineyards.com (707) 944-2770 TF: $$$ Hrs: 10:30 - 3:30 by Appt

This is a charming private winery with great views of Napa's best vineyards. They spent three years re-engineering their land before planting their grapes. The Gargiulo family has a long tradition with agriculture, and they know how to make a great bottle of wine. They do a very relaxed, elegant sit down tasting at specific times with a knowledgeable staff. This part of the valley is home to some of Napa's most prestigious wineries; Silver Oak, Rudd, Groth, Vine Cliff, Harlan, Cardinale and Far Niente. **Map 19**

**Girard Winery** - Downtown Tasting Room - Wines: Cab Sauv, Cab Franc, Petite Sirah, Zin, Chard, Sauv Blanc. 6795 Washington St. Yountville CA 94599 www.girardwinery.com (707) 968-9297 TF: $$ Hrs: 10-6 The

Girard Family has been making wine in Napa for many years and their current property is perched on a hillside in Sage Canyon. They make very good wines and their new lovely tasting room in Yountville is a lot more convenient. They tend to stay open later and that makes them popular late in the day, although the wines should attract people at all hours. **MAP 22**

**Goosecross Cellars** - Yountville Charm - Wines: Viognier, Chenin Blanc, Sauv Blanc, Chard, Orange Muscat, Cab Sauv, Merlot, Cab Franc, Syrah, Red Blends, Meritage. 1119 State Ln. Yountville CA 94599 www.goosecross. com (707) 944-1986 TF: $ Hrs: 10-4:30

This is a small winery, with a great wine selection. You walk past the fermentation tanks and taste in the barrel room. The winemaker is also the vineyard manager. That means he guides the grapes along their entire journey into the bottle. They have a great staff, informal and friendly. They sell etched and chocolate dipped bottles. Goosecross is a favorite among the professional guides, because while they are small, they pour wonderful, well priced wines with a great deal of knowledge and humor. They have a nice gift section and they do wonderful education seminars. **MAP 17**

**Grgich Hills Cellar** - Judgment of Paris Wine Maker  - Wines: Chard, Fumé Blanc, Violetta, Cab Sauv, Zin, Merlot.  1829 St Helena Hwy S (Hwy 29) Rutherford   www.grgich.com   (707) 963-2784   Hrs: 9:30- 4:30 Tours $$ at 11 & 2   TF: $$ (logo glass)

Grgich Hills has a great reputation and what they lack in 'pretty', they make up for with friendly, quality and value. The winery is located just off Hwy 29 and next to the train tracks. The windowless tasting room doubles as the barrel room so it's dark and earthy, but the wines are good and a great value. Mike Grgich (Pronounced Gur Gitch), from Croatia, worked with Beaulieu Vineyard's revered winemaker Andre Tchelistcheff. Later he was the winemaker at Chateau Montelena when they produced the top ranked Chardonnay at the 1976 Judgment of Paris that put Napa on the wine map. A year later, Grgich Hills (named for the Hills Bros. coffee family) was born on July 4th. They own America's largest Biodynamic vineyards managed by Mike's nephew and the winery is managed by his daughter. The tasting room staff is knowledgeable and relaxed, the tasting is reasonable and the experience is thoroughly authentic. This is where the Wine Train stops. **MAP 22**

**Groth Vineyards & Winery** - Big Pink  - Wines: Cab Sauv, Chard, Sauv Blanc. 750 Oakville Cross Rd. Oakville  CA  94562   www.grothvineyards.com (707) 754-4254   TF: $$  CWP   Hrs: 10-4 by Appt

This is a grand building in pink stucco with good wines but an anti-climatic tasting, and not always easy to get on the phone. The place is beautiful and they have a nice staff and the tasting is even reasonable for the quality, but it is a very simple tasting bar amid a grand room. Obviously, the wine club members enjoy the place, but for the casual visitor it feels like the experience is behind glass, just as the barrels are.  **MAP 9**

**Guilliams Vineyards** - Spring Mountain  - Wines: Bordeaux.  3851 Spring Mountain Rd.  St. Helena  CA  94574  (707) 963-9059  TF: $ Hrs: by Appt

This is a very small winery on Spring Mountain that shares its driveway with Charbay. As you come up the driveway, look for the round building. Take your time as you get close, watch the numbers, because it is not the easiest driveway to get into. They make about a 1000 cases so this is for the enthusiasts. They produce lovely, hand wines.  **MAP 12**

**Gustavo Thrace** - Tasting Room by Oxbow - Wines: Cab Sauv, Chard, Sauv Blanc, Barbera, Pinot Noir, Petite Sirah, Bordeaux blends. 1021 McKinstry St. Napa CA 94559 www.Gustavothrace.com (707) 257-6796 TF: $$ Hrs: 11-7 Sun-Wed, 11-9 Thu-Sat. The winemaker is Gustavo Brambila, part of the famous Chateau Montelena team that produced the award winning Chardonnay in 1976 at the Judgment of Paris. He then moved to Grgich Hills Cellars, making wine there for 23 years. This is their tasting room. **MAP 21**

**Hagafen Cellars** - Oak Knoll Kosher - Wines: Riesling, Syrah, Cab Franc. 4160 Silverado Trail Napa CA 94558 www.hagafen.com (707) 252-0781 TF: $ Hrs: 10-5 . This is a nice tasting room with kosher wines that have been served at the White House. It is tucked a little ways off the road in a pretty building with an intimate tasting room. They have a very nice staff and very convenient location, just north of the city of Napa on the Silverado Trail. The word Hagafen is Hebrew for wine. **Map 17**

**Hall Wines** – Wine and Sculpture - Wines: Cab Sauv, Merlot, Sauv Blanc - 401 St Helena Hwy S (Hwy 29). St. Helena CA 94574 They have a second cave location by appointment. www.hallwines.com (707) 967-2626 TF: $$$ Hrs: 10-5:30. This winery is next to Dean & DeLuca, and it recently went through a major transformation into an Architectural wonder that looks more like a museum than a winery, in part explained by the great art collection housed on the site. Very modern and sleek and quite different from their other property on the nountain. They make some good wines and have a very pleasant staff. For the enthusiast, visit their beautiful mountain top winery caves by appointment. This is a more expensive visit, but the views are great and the sit-down tasting is in one Napa's most beautiful caves. It is lined with antique bricks from Austria, and the hallways feature smaller pieces from their sculpture collection. **MAP 22**

**Hans Fahden Vineyards** - Mountain Location. This winery is most popular as an event space. - Wines: Cab Sauv 4855 Petrified Forest Rd Calistoga CA 94515 www.hansfahden.com (707) 942-6760 TF: NA Hrs: by Appt **MAP 10**

**Hartwell Vineyards** - Stags Leap - Wines: Cab Sauv, Merlot. 5795 Silverado Trail Napa CA 94558 www.hartwellvineyards.com (707) 255-4269TF: $$$$ Hrs: by Appt. This is a beautiful winery in the rolling hills of the Stags Leap district. The views looking south down the valley are great. The building has a wonderful Tuscan feel by design, and the winery facility is excellent, as are the wines. There is a tasting bar and a tasting room in the cave with a banquet table, and the whole experience is gracious and enjoyable. They are by appointment. **Map 17**

**Heitz Wine Cellars** - Well Respected Label  - Wines: Cab Sauv, Chard, Grignolino, Rosé, Zin, Port.  436 St Helena Hwy (Hwy 29). S. St. Helena  CA 94574  www.heitzcellar.com  (707) 963-3542  TF: $  Hrs: 11-4:30

This modest tasting room conveniently located just south of downtown St. Helena is the outlet for one of Napa's most respected family wineries. Their wines have a great history, and the vineyards and home ranch are in a canyon off of the Silverado Trail next to the Joseph Phelps winery. The tasting bar is low and comfortable, making less of a barrier between the visitor and the staff. Wonderful wines in a great location near to Hall, Louis M Martini and Prager Port works. **Map 19**

**Hendry Wines** - Northern Edge of Carneros  Navigation Tip: It is 2.5 miles from Highway 29 on the way to the Hess Collection - Wines: Albariño, Pinot Gris, Chard,  Rosé, Pinot Noir, Primitivo, Blends, Zin, Cab Sauv.  3104 Redwood Rd.  Napa CA 94558  www.hendrywines.com  (707) 226-8320  TF: $$$  Hrs: by Appt with tour.

The property has been in the family since the 1930's and there have been vineyards there since the 1860's. They do a great tour of the vineyards and their gravity flow winery reminds us of the format used at Opus One. The tour is often with a family member. You should plan on spending two hours. It is in an area with only a few other wineries. Navigation Tip: It is 2.5 miles from Route 29 on the way to the Hess Collection. **MAP 16**

**Hess Collection Winery** - Great Art Collection in Southern  - Wines: Cab Sauv, Sauv Blanc, Chard, Syrah, Late Harvest Riesling, Malbec, Cab Franc, Syrah Rosé, Petite Sirah, Zin, Sauv Blanc, Viognier, Semillon, Shiraz, Blends, Olive Oil, Vinegar.  4411 Redwood Rd.  Napa  94558  www.hesscollection.com  (707) 255-1144  TF: $$ - $$$$$  Hrs: 10-5:30

This destination winery houses a world class modern art collection on several floors of an historic stone barn, facing another barn that houses a state of the art winery. Hess has vineyards around California and offers a wide line of products, but many high end wines are only available here at the winery. The tasting room and gift shop are worth seeing by themselves. Great tour. The barns are classic historic Napa and owned by the Christian Brothers Winery who have their center next door. Hess is located on Mount Veeder in the southwest corner of Napa, north of Carneros. The ride there on Redwood road is winding and a bit out of the way. If it wasn't for the outstanding art collection the winery might not get as much traffic, but the winery experience is impressive and they stay pleasantly busy. **MAP 16**

**Hill Family Estate** - Downtown Tasting Room  - Wines: Chard, Pinot Noir, Merlot, Cab Sauv, Syrah.  6512 Washington Street, Yountville  CA  94599  www.hillfamilyestate.com  (707) 944-9580  TF: $$ CWP  Hrs: 10-6

Their tasting room is right in the center of Yountville, but don't let the location hide the fact that this is a winery with a great deal of depth. They own numerous, excellent vineyards around Napa, and have been selling grapes to top wineries for many years, while running a vineyard management company. This is a Mom and Pop and the kids business, and they produce a great product at a surprisingly reasonable price. The secret to wine pricing often relates to how much people paid for their land, and the Hills have owned their land for a good long while. Besides the fun tasting in town, they also host events at their ranch. These are wonderful folks and authentic Napa. **MAP 22**

**Honig Cellars** - By Appt  - Wines: Sauv Blanc, Cab Sauv - 850 Rutherford Rd.  Rutherford  CA  94573   www.honigcellars.com   (707) 963-5618  TF: $$ - $$$  Hrs: 10-4 by Appt

Their tasting patio is relaxed and stylish, and the mood is entertaining and gracious. They also do a more private, reserve tasting inside at a conference table. It is a serious look at their library wines, and it gives you a chance to realize that they own some very good vineyards in Rutherford. This is a family business in their third generation and the younger generation still brings a lot of enthusiasm to the game. **Map 19**

**Hopper Creek Winery/ Noah** - Eccentric and Fun  - Wines: Chard, Merlot, Cab Sauv,  Zin.  6204 Washington Street  Yountville CA 94599   www. hoppercreek.com (707) 944-0675  TF: $  Hrs: 11-4 Tues-Sun (instant Appt) This is a very small winery on the same road as Bell Winery, just south of Yountville. It is a bit rustic, but the inside of the tasting room is eccentric and fun. **Map 17**

**Inglenook**- AKA Rubicon Estate - Napa Italian Style with History owned by Coppola  - Wines: Chard, Cab Sauv, Merlot, Cab Franc, Syrah, Blanc de Blanc, Rosé, Sauv Blanc, Pinot Noir, Zin, Rubicon.  1991 St Helena Hwy (Hwy 29). Rutherford  94573      www.rubiconestate.com   (707) 968-1100  Hrs: 10-5 TF: $$$$$  with various tours

This is the premier winery of the movie director Francis Ford Coppola where they produce their best estate wines. It includes a spacious tasting room, an elegant gift shop and an espresso bar, which is a wonderful place to relax amid a day of tasting with some chocolate or a cigar; which they sell in the cafe.  You can sail a boat in the fountain making this among the most family-friendly wineries in Napa. The staff is excellent and the whole feeling is gracious and special. The Inglenook building is on the National Register of Historic Places in the San Francisco Bay Area. It was the center of the Niebaum Estate that Francis gradually reassembled. 'Rubicon' comes from the story of Julius Caesar returning from Gaul after his victories there. His enemies rigged the laws against him so crossing the Rubicon River into Italy would make him a rebel. Once he crossed, there was no going back. Once Francis made his first wine there was no going back. **Map 19**

**James Cole Estate Winery** - Oak Knoll District  - Wines: Chard, Malbec, Cab Sauv, Ice Wine.  5014 Silverado Trail  Napa  CA  94558    www.james-colewinery.com  (707) 251-9905   TF: $  Hrs: 10-5

They are located at the intersection of the Silverado Trail and Oak Knoll Road, owned by a local family. The tasting is casual, the staff friendly and knowledgeable, and the wines very good. The building and tasting room are elegant and understated. When the Trail wineries are busy, you might find a nicer experience here, away from the crowds. **Map 17**

**Jarvis Vineyards** - Remarkable Cave Winery  - Wines: Chard, Cab Sauv, Malbec, Merlot, Petit Verdot, Cab Franc.   2970 Monticello Rd.  Napa  CA  94558  www.jarviswines.com  (800) 255-5280   TF: $$$$$  with Tour  Hrs: 11-4:30 by Appt at 10-11-1-2-3

The winery is entirely inside their beautiful cave and tasting there is a unique experience, as you cross over a stream that runs through the caves. They have an event space filled with museum quality crystals, but bring a sweater as it can get a bit chilly. There is a 24 hour cancellation policy. The drive out Monticello Road is a little long and winding but very beautiful. Look for a rock outcropping just before you get there that looks like a man smoking a pipe. **MAP 6**

**Jessup Cellars** - Downtown Tasting Room   - Wines: Chard, Rosé, Merlot, Zin, Cab Sauv, Blends, Petite Sirah, Zin Port.   6740 Washington St. Yountville CA 94599  www.jessupcellars.com    (707) 944-8523    TF: $$ CWP Hrs: 10-6  They are popular with small tour companies so their tasting room can get filled up fast, but it's still fun. Some wonderful wines and the space doubles as an art gallery. Their vineyards are on Atlas Peak, and they also source grapes from Mount Veeder and other areas. **MAP 22**

**Joseph Phelps Vineyards** - Beautiful Valley   Navigation Tip: Their street, Taplin Road, is on the east side of the Silverado Trail just north of the intersection with Zinfandel Lane.

It is a tight turn and the first part of the road is narrow so take your time.- Wines: Cab Sauv, Sauv Blanc, Syrah, Viognier, Dessert Wine.  200 Taplin Rd.  St. Helena  CA  94574  www.jpvwines.com  (707) 967-3720  TF: $$$ - $$$$  Hrs: 9-5  Mon-Fri   10-4  Sat-Sun  by appt
They sit in their own valley just off the Silverado Trail. They offer tastings and seminars by appointment. Their lovely tasting room with patio is being renovated in 2014 but their wines are highly respected. They have a very knowledgeable and relaxed staff and beautiful grounds.

They were the first Napa winery to create a Bordeaux-style blend; that mix of Cabernet Sauvignon, Merlot, Cabernet Franc, that is the world standard. Their signature blend, Insignia, was voted the world's top wine several years ago. **MAP 9**

**Judd's Hill Winery** - Custom Crush - Wines: Cab Sauv, Petite Sirah, Chard, Merlot, Zin, Pinot Noir. 2332 Silverado Trail Napa CA 94558 www.juddshill.com (707) 255-2332 TF: $$ Hrs: 10-5 by Appt

This is a fun place, although a bit chaotic. That is because they are also a custom facility. Unlike the many that exist throughout wine country, they work with clients as small as one barrel, which is very tempting. They near the intersection of the southern Silverado Trail and Trancas Street. **Map 17**

**Kelham Vineyards & Winery** - True Napa - Wines: Cab Sauv, Sauv Blanc, Merlot, Chard, Port. 360 Zinfandel Ln. St. Helena CA 94574 www.kelhamvineyards.com (707) 963-2000 TF: $$$ Hrs: by Appt

This is a gracious, charming family run winery. They do a sit down tasting outside on a remarkable patio. Inside is a most unique art collection. The pieces were created by a French artist who works with the foil capsules from the wine bottles to make figures related to the wineries. They are very elegant and the Kelham's offer a number of these art pieces for sale. The tasting is almost always done by the family, including Ronald and Hamilton, the two winemakers. They are by appointment, but if you appreciate great wines and want to visit the best of Napa, call them. By the way, they have the friendliest dogs in the valley. They have beautiful architecture and gardens. **MAPS 7 & 9**

**Kuleto Estate Family Vineyards** - Top of Sage Canyon - Wines: Cab Sauv, Sangiovese, Syrah, Pinot Noir, Rosato, Chard 2470 Sage Canyon Rd. St. Helena CA 94574 www.kuletoestate.com (707) 963-9750 TF: $$$$ Hrs: Mon-Sat by Appt

This is by appointment and the guests receive a map and gate code upon confirmation. It is already quite a ride out Sage Canyon Road before you get to the gate. Then it is a long winding driveway with 12 convex mirrors at the hairpin turns that brings you up to the winery. Amazingly, it is worth the trip, because the site is great, the vineyards are perched on top of the mountains, the buildings are unique, with a great sense of muscularity and grace. They have wonderful, working antique cars and trucks, and a great staff. This is a popular place for events and groups to come. **MAP 20**

**Ladera** - Historic Howell Mountain - Wines: Cab Sauv, Blends. 150 White Cottage Rd. S. Angwin CA 94508 www.laderavineyards.com (707) 965-2445 TF: $$ - $$$ Hrs: Tours & Tasting by Appt Mon- Sat

The original building was constructed in 1886 and renovated by the new owners in 2000. They make about 10,000 cases a year using gravity fed methods and mostly native yeast. They do private tours by appointment for which you should allow an hour. There is a lot of history on Howell Mountain, and a whole bunch of it is centered on Ladera. They offer tastings at 11, 1 & 3. Tours at: 10, 12 , 2, all by appointment. **MAP 13**

**Laird Family Estate** - Oak Knoll Copper Pyramid  - Wines: Pinot Grigio, Chard, Syrah, Cab Sauv, Merlot.  5055 Solano Ave.  Napa  CA  94558   www.lairdfamilyestate.com   (707) 257-0360  TF: $$  CWP  Hrs: 10-5

This is a unique building, a pyramid, with a nice surrounding patio and flowers. Part of the activity that you see there comes from their role as a custom crush facility for many other smaller wineries. The Laird family has a long history growing grapes in Napa. They have a cool tasting room and good wines, but because so much of their business is about their custom crush customers, who are not poured there, you get the sense that the tasting room is a bit of an afterthought. **Map 17**

**Larkmead Vineyards** - Calistoga by Appointment  - Wines: Cab Sauv, Merlot, Sauv Blanc.  1100 Larkmead Ln.  Calistoga CA  94515  www.larkmead.com   (707) 942-0167   TF: $$$   Hrs: 10-4 by Appt

This winery is easy to spot as you travel north on Hwy 29 above St. Helena. It is a bright, white building complex with a homey, but modern style. They are a quality producer and the family, which has long ties in San Francisco, has owned the vineyards for many years. They opened to the public only recently and their permit allows them limited, by appointment tastings, so call in advance.  They do a lovely sit down tasting in their salon-like tasting room with great views of the vineyards. **MAP 10**

**Lava Vine** - Tasting Room  - Wines: Chard, Cab Sauv, Syrah.  965 Silverado Trail Calistoga  CA  94515  www.lavavine.com   (707) 942-9500   TF: $$, Hrs: 10-5.  This is a new winery that gets its name from the fact that its vineyards are located on an old lava flow.  Much of the northern valley was volcanic three to four million years ago, and that rocky soil is one of the elements that make the area so good for the Bordeaux-style wines. They are just five minutes from downtown Calistoga. The tasting room is in a separate building behind the house that faces the street. It probably was a garage at one time. Inside the tasting bar can accommodate a dozen people easily, and it makes a wonderfully social place to enjoy their wines. **MAP 10**

**LMR Farmstead Tasting Room & Restaurant**  - Wines: Cab Sauv, Sauv Blanc, Sangiovese, Ranch House Red, Olive Oil, Beef Jerky. 738 Main St. St Helena CA  94574 - Winery 1775 Whitehall Ln. St. Helena CA  94574 www.longmeadowranch.com    (707) 963-4555   TF: $$ - $$$$$ (w/tour) 11-6 Hrs: by Appt

This is not the winery that you can visit in a casual way since it always includes at least an hour and a half tour, starting in their four wheel drive troop transport. They pick you up at their farm market on Highway 29, the LMR Rutherford Gardens. They also have a new tasting room and restaurant called the Farmstead conveniently located near downtown St. Helena. The main property is a 650 acre farm and winery, producing not only wine and olive oil, but also produce and meats. The winery buildings are beautiful and the location, on the hillsides overlooking the valley, is great. As you drive north on Highway 29 you can see them to your left as you pass Whitehall Lane. They are Biodynamic and Organic. They also breed and sell horses. This is very much a complete experience. **MAP 23**

**Louis M. Martini Winery** - Great Wines in Central Napa - Wines: Cab Sauv, old vine Zin, Chard, Merlot, Cab Franc, Syrah, Petite Sirah, Late Harvest Moscato, Meritage. 254 St Helena Hwy S. (Hwy 29). St. Helena 94574 (800) 321-9463 www.louismartini.com Hrs: 10-6, TF: $$ - $$$, Tours by Appt

This is proof that you can't judge a book by its cover, because the first impression of Louis M Martini is an industrial, ceramic brick faced warehouse, leading to a dark brown entranceway. But, once you get inside, this stylish, gracious winery, with a sleek, modern tasting room leads into one of Napa's most inviting Italian-style gardens, with tables for tasting, entertaining and picnics. All of this is nicely away from the noise of the road and the glare of the Sun. The staff is unfailingly knowledgeable and accommodating. Even though many people know them for their less expensive wines, their high end wine's reputation is excellent. Their southern Sonoma Monte Rosso vineyards are considered some of California's best, producing famous old vine Zinfandel. If you like BIG REDS this is the place for you. The winery is in its third generation, and is still managed by the family, even though it was purchased by the Gallo family, who are long-time friends. They also do cave tours and reserve tastings. **MAP 18**

**Luna Vineyards** - Elegant Southern Silverado - Wines: Merlot, Napa Valley Cab Sauv, Sangiovese, Pinot Grigio. 2921 Silverado Trail Napa CA 94558 www.lunavineyards.com (707) 255-5862 TF: $$ - $$$ Hrs: 10-5

They are located at the southern end of the Silverado Trail making them very convenient for day trips. They have a gorgeous, comfortable tasting room surrounded by a shaded porch, complete with beautiful outdoor furniture. They do special tours and tastings by appointment and have an elegant gift area plus they make seriously good wines. They started off with a focus on Italian wines, and while they produce and distribute a popular Pinot Grigio, they often don't pour it in the tasting room. Now they are much bigger in the Bordeaux-style wines. Wines: Merlot, Napa Valley Cabernet Sauvignon, Sangiovese, Pinot Grigio. Navigation Tip: They are one of the first wineries that you encounter on the left hand side as you go north on the Silverado Trail. If you are planning a brief tour then from here you have Darioush, Black Stallion, Signorello and Reynolds all nearby. **Map 17**

**Madonna Estate** - Carneros - Wines: Pinot Grigio, Chard, Pinot Noir, Merlot, Dolcetto, Cab Sauv, Riesling, Gewürztraminer, Muscat Canelli. 5400 Old Sonoma Rd. Napa CA 94559 www.madonnaestate.com (707) 255-8864

TF: $ - $$ includes logo glass  Hrs: 10-5

This is an organic winery with dry farmed vineyards, which is pretty unusual. They have a picnic area just off the road. They are very convenient from San Francisco which makes them a popular tour bus stop. They are 3rd & 4th generation Italian-American winemakers, and they make remarkably good wines that are properly priced. If there isn't a tour bus in their lot then they are worth a visit. Very nice staff! **MAP 15**

**Ma(i)sonry** - Collective Tasting Room and Design Center  6711 Washington Street Yountville CA 94599  www.maisonry.com  (707) 944-0889  TF: $$$  Hrs: 10-7.

This is a combination tasting room/design center that pours for small production, high end wineries. The tastings are by appointment, sitting down, although if it is slow consider walking in for an instant appointment. The tasting is expensive, but it is worth visiting to see the furniture and environment. They have a great outdoor area and many unique features. They are right across the street from Jessup Winery and nearby the Girard Winery. **MAP 22**

**Markham Vineyards** - Rock and Roll  - Wines: Merlot, Cab Sauv, Sauv Blanc, Chard. 2812 St Helena Hwy N. (Hwy 29) St. Helena CA 94574  www.markhamvineyards.com (707) 963-5292  TF: $$ - $$$  Hrs: 11-5

This winery is located north of downtown St. Helena. It is a well known producer of middle of the road wines. They have a spacious tasting room with an art gallery featuring photography of Rock & Roll icons from the 60's and 70's, a nice gift shop and some good, well-priced wines. Their staff is always pleasant and the grounds and patio are a pleasant place to hangout. **MAP 10**

**Marston Family Winery** - Spring Mountain  - Wines: Cab Sauv.  Sulphur Springs Rd  St Helena CA 94574  www.marstonfamilyvineyard.com  (707) 260-4692  TF: PIE  Hrs: Appt.

This property 150 years was a resort that hosted famous people. Like much of this volcanic area, its medicinal hot springs drew people from all over. You can still smell sulfur when you pass by. Their first commercial vintage was in 1998. They produce a high end Cabernet Sauvignon by appointment and for the collector. **MAP 4**

**Mayacamas Winery** - Mountain Adventures  - Wines: Cab Sauv, Chard, Sauv Blanc, Pinot Noir.  1155 Lokoya Rd.  Napa CA 94558  www.mayacamas.com  (707) 224-4030  TF: PIE  Hrs: Appt Mon-Fri

This winery is in a remote location reached via gravel roads, 35 minutes from the valley floor. It sits on the rim of an extinct volcano and it is by appointment during the week.  The winery was started in 1889 and the highest vineyards are at 2300 feet, which is very high for Napa. The winemaking style is very different from most of new oak-crazed Napa. The tanks are neutral and the barrels are old. The thin soil and cool winds make for great acidity, making wines that need to age before they are ready to drink. It is a unique experience. **MAP 16**

**McKensie Mueller** - Carneros Appointment- Wines: Pinot, Chard - 2530 Las Amigas Rd   Napa CA 94559  www.McKensieMueller.com  (707) 252-0186 TF: PIE  Hrs: By Appt  **MAP 15**

**Merryvale Vineyards** - Downtown Winery - Wines: Sauv Blanc, Chard, Merlot, Cab Sauv, Fortified Dessert Wine, Zin, Pinot Noir.   1000 Main St. St. Helena  CA  94574  www.merryvale.com   (707) 963-7777  TF: $$ - $$$ Hrs: 10-6:30
        This building was once owned by the Mondavi family during the days of bulk winemaking. It sits beside the railroad tracks, and they would pull the tanker cars up to the doors of the barrel room and fill them up. Now that grand room, lined with ancient, huge barrels is used for events, with a banquet table running the length of it. They have a big tasting bar, a great gift section, and a very festive tasting room that is open late compared to their neighbors. The tasting room is adjacent to the winery's tank room and you can see the line of stainless tanks through the doorway.
   They are walking distance to downtown St Helena and next to the restaurants Tra Vigne, Pizzeria Tra Vigne & Taylor's Refresher. The wines are first rate and this is a popular place. **MAP 18**

**Michael Mondavi Winery SOLD** - 1285 Dealy Ln.  Napa CA 94559 www.michaelmondavifamilyestate.com  (707) 256-2757  TF: $$-$$$   Hrs: 11-5.  This is a pretty place with very pleasant tasting rooms in the Carneros District near Artesa. They recently were sold and when we have the new infor we will add it to the App first and then the book. **MAP 15**

**Milat Vineyards Winery** - Small Family Owned  - Wines: Chenin Blanc, Chard, Merlot, Zin, Cab Sauv, Port, Chocolate Port Sauce.   1091 St Helena Hwy (Hwy 29). S  St. Helena  CA  94574   www.milat.com   (707) 963-0758 TF: $  CWP Hrs: 10-5:30   This is a small, family-owned winery that produces very good wines at reasonable prices. The tasting room, just off of Route 29, is small but very convenient. **Map 19**

**Miner Family Vineyards** - Great Views  - Wines: Chard, Viognier, Sauv Blanc, Cab Sauv, Pinot Noir, Merlot, Syrah, Zin, Sangiovese, Rosato.   7850 Silverado Trail  Oakville  CA  94558  www.minerwines.com  (707) 944-9500 TF: $ - $$  Hrs: 11-5. This is a fun winery with a very interesting list made from grapes they source both inside and outside Napa. They have great views from the front patio and a friendly staff. You can see the entire winery from above and they have a cave out back that they use for events.  **Map 19**

**Monticello Cellars** - Oak Knoll - Wines: Cab Sauv, Merlot, Blend. 4242 Big Ranch Rd. Napa CA 94558 www.CorleyFamilyNapaValley.com (707) 253-2802 TF: $$ - $$$ Hrs: 10-4:30

They are located in the southern part of the valley just north of Downtown Napa, in the Oak Knoll district. This area produces some very nice wines and they are nearby the Andretti winery and Trefethen. They are also the site of a scaled replica of the home of Thomas Jefferson, Monticello, although the bar tastings are done in a facing building, they do the high end tasting in the cellar under Monticello and it is very nice. They have a nice picnic area although they suggest you reserve your table. **Map 17**

**Mumm Napa** - Sparkling Wines & Great Photo Gallery - Wines: Sparkling & Still Wines. 8445 Silverado Trail Rutherford 94573 www.mummnapa. com (707) 967-7700 Hrs: 10-5 TF: $ - $$$ by glass or flight

This is a fun winery where they pour great sparkling wines both inside their glass walled tasting room and outside on their expansive patio. It is a sit down tasting and they have a talent for finding great, friendly staff. The location, tucked against the eastern side of the valley on the Silverado Trail, gives the winery great views and a central location. They pour unusual, fun sparkling wines, very different from the classical approach. They have a nice gift shop and a fantastic photography museum, with rotating exhibits and they offer free tours. Even though most of their vineyards are to the south in Carneros, the founding winemaker chose this site for its beauty and reminded everyone that he had trucks to move the grapes. **Map 19**

**Napa Cellars** - Friendly Winery - Wines: Chard, Sauv Blanc, Zin, Cab Sauv, Merlot, Pinot Noir, Syrah. Picnic tables. 7481 St. Helena Highway Hwy 29 Oakville CA 94562 www.NapaCellars.com (707) 944-2565 TF: $ - $$ Hrs: 10-6. They share the tasting room with Folie a Deux in a very convenient location just north of Yountville and they're open to 6 pm. They enjoy the loyalty of a young clientele and it makes the place a lot of fun. **Map 19**

**Napa Wine Company** - Collective Winery 7830-40 St Helena Hwy (Hwy 29). Oakville CA 94558 www.napawineco.com (707) 944-1710 TF: varies Hrs: 10-4:30. This is one of Napa's oldest bonded wineries, and they are known for the cult wineries that use their custom crush facility. The wines that are poured in the tasting room are made at the winery and it includes some serious players. Although, like all group tasting rooms, the list of wines that they offer changes over time. They ask that groups of 6 or more call ahead. It is a nice tasting room and they are very conveniently located at the corner of Oakville Road and Highway 29. **Map 19**

**Neal Family Vineyards** - Howell Mountain - Wines: Cab Sauv, Sauv Blanc, Petite Syrah, Zin. 716 Liparita Road Angwin CA 94508 www.nealvine-

yards.com   (707) 965-2800    TF: PIE    Hrs: 10-5 by Appt
This is a very small production, high quality, state of the art winery. They are a little bit of a drive up mountainous winding roads, but if you are an enthusiast then it is worth it. Like many small wineries, they offer a tour. **MAP 13**

**Newton Vineyard** - Napa's Best Gardens  - Wines: Chard, Merlot, Cab Sauv, Cab Franc, Petit Verdot.   2555 Madrona Ave.  St. Helena  CA  94574  www. newtonvineyard.com   (707) 963-9000  TF: $$$   Hrs: Appt.

They have remarkable gardens and the views from the ridges of Spring Mountain are some of the best around, in fact, there are numerous photos from that location in our books. They are one of the few Spring Mountain wineries that are reached from the valley floor. They have a very nice staff and great wines, but the tasting and tour schedule is a bit limited so you have to plan ahead. The architecture is very interesting, with much of the production winery in caves in the hillsides. The original owner loved ornamental gardens and these are some of Napa's best. The winery is Biodynamic. Plan on 15 minutes to get there from downtown St. Helena, then plan on an hour and a half for the tour and tasting. They are always combined. **MAP 12**

**Nichelini Winery** - Chiles Valley  - Wines: Sauv Vert, Chard, Zin, Petite Sirah, Cab Sauv, Primitivo.   2950 Sage Canyon Rd.  St. Helena  CA  94574 www.nicheliniwinery.com  (707) 963-0717  TF: $  Hrs: 10-5 weekends

This is one of Napa's oldest family wineries perched on a hillside in the Chiles Valley (rhymes with tiles) and are opened primarily on the weekends. It is a twenty minute ride from the Silverado Trail out Sage Canyon Road, but more than worth it, especially in the summertime. In the winter, it gets cold up there, so wear a jacket and call ahead. They make wonderful wine in a great location. When you see where they are and realize that the original settlers did much of this work by hand, it is amazing. They have Bocce courts and a picnic area. **MAP 20**

**Nickel & Nickel** - Oakville Charm by Appointment  - Wines: Chard, Cab Sauv, Merlot, Syrah, Zin.    8164 St Helena Hwy (Hwy 29).  Oakville  CA 94558  www.nickelandnickel.com   (707) 967-9600   TF: $$$$  Hrs: 10-3 by Appt.  They have beautiful buildings and gardens, and a great tour and sit-down tasting of their single vineyard wines. They are associated with Far Niente, and when you make an appointment with one, if it is booked, they can check on the other for you. They also do just tastings but the site is so cool that you should do the tour if you can. The winery sits across from the Robert Mondavi Winery and you can spot it from the horses grazing in front of the house.  **Map 19**

**O'Brien Family Vineyard** - Seduction Wine  - Wines: Chard, Merlot, Bordeaux Blend called Seduction.   1200 Orchard Ave.  Napa CA  94558    www.

obrienfamilyvineyard.com  (707) 252-8463  TF: $$$  CWP    Hrs: 10 to 5
Tue-Sun call for Appt.  This is a family winery on a beautiful property that is
very convenient to downtown Napa. They do a very good tour, romantic and
personal and a wine tasting sitting in the vineyards. The winery equipment is
right next to the tasting room. The wines are quite special, as are the people
who make it. Their vineyards are Biodynamic/Organic. **Map 17**

**Odette Estate** - Pretty Winery  - Wines: A mix of classic Napa varietals from
their other wineries, Plumpjack and Cade.   5998 Silverado Trail  Napa  CA
94558   Hrs: 10:30 to 4   www.OdetteEstate.com  (707) 224-7533
This was the former Stelzner property which was bought by the Plumpjack
group and they are gradually transforming it into something that we think will
be remarkable. **MAP 17**

**Opus One Winery** - An International Standard  - Wines: Bordeaux style
Blend.   7900 St Helena Hwy (Hwy 29).   Oakville 94562     www.OpusOne-
Winery.com (707) 944-9442  TF: $$$$$  Hrs: 10-4  by Appt, Tour by Appt
     Opus One is an 'expense account wine' found on wine lists around the
world and sure to impress any client that you're entertaining. This extraordi-
nary building is styled after an Incan temple, a white exterior submerged into
green lawns surrounded by vines which are grown in the European method.
It was started in the 1970's by the Baron Von Rothschild and Robert Mondavi
to combine European technology and California grapes. They produce about
25,000 cases yearly of one Bordeaux style red wine made from the five clas-
sic varietals, Cabernet Sauvignon, Merlot, Cabernet Franc, Malbec and Petite
Verdot. You enter through the lobby where you sign in. Although tastings are
by appointment, if it's slow day an instant appointment is possible. Tours are
always by appointment, and the high-end tours are great. The tasting is one
generous pour, although they normally offer a choice of two vintages. They
have a small, beautifully appointed tasting room, but if the weather is nice,
and it usually is, go upstairs to the loggia which offers beautiful views of the
valley. **Map 19**

**Orin Swift Cellars** - New Downtown Tasting Room Location  - Wines: Cab-
ernet, Syrah. 1321 (?) Main St.  St Helena (Hwy 29) CA 94574  www.orins-
wift.com  (707) 976-9179  TF: PIE   Hrs: Appt    **MAP 23**

**O'Shaughnessy** Estate Winery - Howell Mountain  - Wines: Cab Sauv, Mer-
lot. Friesen Dr  Angwin  CA  94508  www.oshaughnessywinery.com  (707)
965-2898  TF: PIE  Hrs: by appt. Double Check to make sure they are there.
     This is a beautiful, although isolated winery north east of the town of
Angwin. Their first vintage was in 2000. They get very high ratings and, if you
are an enthusiast, it is well worth the effort to make the appointment and ac-
tually find the place. Get them to email you the directions because it is a maze

of small roads that you have navigate to find them. **MAP 13**

**Outpost Wines** - Howell Mountain  - Wines: Zin, Grenache, Petite Sirah, Cab Sauv.  2075 Summit Lake Dr.  Angwin  CA  94508  www.outpostwines. com  (707) 965-1718   TF: $$$   Hrs: by Appt

They sit on the top of Howell Mountain looking across at Spring Mountain on the other side of the Valley. While they produce some wonderful wines, they are known just as much as a crush facility for some of Napa's hot labels. It is quite a ride to the top, but the views and the wines are great. Get them to send you directions. **MAP 13**

**Palmaz Vineyards** - The Biggest Caves  - Wines: Cab Sauv Blends, Riesling, Chard, Muscat Cannelli.   4029 Hagen Road Napa  CA  94559  www.palmaz-vineyards.com(707) 2265587   TF: $$$$$   Hrs: by Appt

This is one of the largest cave wineries in Napa at five stories high. They are located to the east of town in an area that, for some reason, has a number of great wineries in caves. The equipment is state of the art and then some. It is a spectacular site with great views. It is family run and they make seriously good wines and do a great tasting experience. Spanish is also spoken by the family which is originally from Argentina. **MAP 6**

**Paloma Vineyard** - Spring Mountain  - Wines: Merlot -  4013 Spring Mountain Rd. St. Helena CA  94574  www.palomavineyards.com   (707) 963-7504  TF: PIE   Hrs: by Appt. This is a small winery on top of Spring Mountain. They have great views and very steep vineyards. They actually have to hold on to the trellis wires in order to work the vines. They get wonderful reviews for their wines and the tasting is on the patio of their house with the owners. This is a winery for the enthusiast. **MAP 12**

**Paoletti Vineyards** - Italian Style  - Wines: Bordeaux and Super Tuscan blends, Nero d' Avola (Sicilian varietal similar to a new world Shiraz), Rose of Sangiovese. 4501 Silverado Trail  Calistoga  CA  94515  www.giannipaoletti. com  (707) 942-0689  TF: $$ with glass  Hrs: 10-5 by Appt

This is a great building with caves and an Italian-style, complete with marble sculptures. The property sits at a curve on the Silverado Trail. They do a nice sit-down tasting for a group by appointment. Being Italians from the restaurant world, they lean towards the Italian varietals. **MAP 10**

**Paradigm Winery** - By Appointment - Wines: Merlot, Cab Sauv, Zin, Cab Franc. 683 Dwyer Rd.  Oakville  CA  94562  www.paradigmwinery.com (707) 944-1683  TF: PIE  Hrs: by Appt

This is a well respected winery just a short ride off of Route 29. They only do tours and tastings during the week at 11 and 2 by appointment. The building and grounds are understated and the tasting room is basic. It is not the easiest winery to make an appointment with, but the wines and staff are very good. The sign at the beginning of Dwyer Road says, "No Wineries this Road". Don't believe everything you read! **Map 19**

**Paraduxx** - Pair of Ducks - Wines: Bordeaux Blends, Cabernet/Zin, Rhone twist blend.  7257 Silverado Trail  Yountville CA  94558  www.paraduxx.com (707) 945-0890  TF: $$$ - $$$$ w/cheese plate.  Hrs: 11-4  by Appt .

This winery sits by itself just off the Silverado Trail north of the intersection with Yountville Cross Road. The name means 'a Pair of Ducks' because it was started by the Duckhorn family to feature their Cabernet/Zinfandel blend. The family sold their three wineries, Duckhorn, Paraduxx and Goldeneye,  although they are still involved in their management. They do a sit-down tasting with a food pairing by appointment. The buildings and grounds are very nice, with indoor and outdoor seating. **Map 19**

**Patz & Hall** - Moved - Wines: Pinot Noir, Chard.  www.patzhall.com  (707) 265-7700  TF: $$$$  Hrs: 10-4.  They are located in a corporate park in southern Napa. They closed their tasting room in Napa where the Trinitas Reserve room is now located and now do their tastings at their winery on 8th Strteet in Sonoma. They source their grapes from various places and their winery facility has always been in Sonoma.

**Peju** Province Winery - A Rutherford Jewel  - Wines: Sauv Blanc, Chard, French Colombard, Syrah, Merlot, Cab Franc, Zin, Cab Sauv, Blends.   8466 St Helena Hwy (Hwy 29) Rutherford  CA  94558   www.peju.com  (707) 963-3600  TF: $- $$  Hrs: 10-6. They are unusual in that they are open to the public, but guests are brought into the tasting in groups, as space is available. On busy days, you should be prepared to wait. This is great place to visit; the grounds are fun, sprinkled about with wonderful sculptures commissioned by the owners, and an abundance of beautiful plantings. The building and rooms inside are beautiful and the gift shop is neat. Groups of 8 or more should call ahead. The wines are well made and often sourced from Pope Valley. Our suggestion is to visit here early before they get busy and you have to wait, because they do a fun tasting. **Map 19**

**Piña Cellars** - Hillside Winery  - Wines: Cab Sauv, 5 Cabernets from 5 vineyards. 8060 Silverado Trail  Rutherford CA  94573       www.pinacellars.com (707) 738-9328, TF: $$  Hrs: 10:00-4:30

This is a very small winery with very good wines. The family runs a long-time vineyard management company so they grow very good grapes, some of which are on the hillsides just above the small winery. The tasting room is also the barrel room, and they have to pull the fork truck out to do the tastings. This is a fun experience and the staff is knowledgeable and involved in the winemaking process. **Map 19**

**Pine Ridge Vineyards** - Stags Leap District - Wines: Chenin Blanc/ Viognier Blend, Rosé, Merlot, Cab Franc, Malbec, Cab Sauv. 5901 Silverado Trail Napa CA 94558 www.pineridgevineyards.com (800) 575-9777 TF: $$ Hrs: 10:30-4:30. This winery sits in its own pretty canyon convenient to many other good wineries. The grounds are lovely, although the best sections are reserved for the wine club members. The tasting room is spacious and connected to the barrel room, which can be seen through the glass doors. The staff is good as are the wines. **Map 17**

**Plumpjack Winery** - Small Winery Big Wines - Wines: Cab Sauv, Merlot, Chard, Syrah. 620 Oakville Cross Rd. Oakville 94558 www.plumpjack.com (707) 945-1220 Hrs: 10-4 8 or more req appt. TF: $$-$$$
You can't ask for a better location than this, just off the Oakville Cross Road, across from Silver Oak, next door to Rudd, and around the corner from Screaming Eagle, all ultra-premium winemakers. Their sign is at the bottom of the hill on the eastern part of the cross road. The narrow driveway goes through the vines to this popular, charming tasting room. The staff is young and fun, the wines are excellent and the prices range from reasonable to serious collector. They are one of the few wineries that use screw caps on some of their high end wines. They have a great gift area right next to the tasting bar which makes it interesting for the members of the party who are running out of tasting endurance. Outside the back door are shaded tables to relax at next to the vines. The winery equipment is across the courtyard from the tasting room, so during the crush in late August through November there is a lot to see. The winery's name and emblematic signs have an old English theme related to Shakespeare and Queen Elizabeth. **Map 19**

**Pope Valley Winery** - Quite a ride to Pope Valley - Wines: Chenin Blanc, Sangiovese, Sangiovese Rosé, Zin, Merlot, Cab Sauv, Zin Port - 6613 Pope Valley Rd. CA 94567 www.popevalleywinery.com (707) 965-1246 TF: $ Hrs: 11-5 Thu-Sun Appt Mon-Wed
This is a small winery that is way out there, 30 minutes over the mountains from the valley floor in the Pope Valley. Due to politics, Pope Valley is considered part of Napa Valley, so many Napa wineries source grapes from this area. This winery dates from 1897 and they manage to stay open during prohibition by selling wine (under the table) to Al Capone and his associates. It is very relaxed with a wide variety of well made, properly priced wines. It's a bit of a ride but worth the trip. One warning: It gets hot in Pope Valley so save this trip for a cooler day. **MAP 13**

**Porter Family Vineyards** - East Napa Caves - Wines: Bordeaux, Sirah- 1189 Green Valley Rd Napa - www.PorterFamilyVineyards.com (707) 265-7980 TF: PIE Hrs: Appt A very beautiful winery in the hills that does private tastings by appointment in their cave which is covered with vines. **MAP 6**

**Prager Winery** & Port Works - Fun and Cozy - Wines: Late Harvest Riesling, Petit Sirah, Port. 1281 Lewelling Ln. St. Helena CA 94574 www.pragerport.com (707) 963-7678 TF: $ Hrs: Mon-Sat 10:30-4:30.

This is a cozy, eccentric tasting room that is popular and fun! They are very much a family business with a very loyal customer base. Tasting there is less like a tasting bar and more like enjoying a favorite port in your uncle's den. The tasting room is papered with money. Their entranceway is a bit hard to find, they are right across the street from Louis M. Martini. **MAP 18**

**Pride Mountain Vineyards** - Stunning Views - Wines: Merlot, Cab Sauv, Cab Franc, Viognier, Chard. 4026 Spring Mountain Rd. St. Helena CA 94574 www.pridewines.com (707) 963-4949 TF: $$ Hrs: Tours & tastings by Appt Wed-Sat, Mon

This beautiful winery sits on the top of Spring Mountain. It is made up of rolling hills that enjoy spectacular views and produce great wines. They also have one of the best picnic areas around that they make available to their customers. They are by appointment so don't bother making the trip there without one. Allow 25 minutes to drive from downtown St Helena. It is a very steep, winding road, so go slow and open your windows so you can hear around the corners! The buildings are beautiful inside and out, the caves are neat, they have a few gifts (including the 'I survived my drive to Pride Mountain Tee shirts) and they do tours by appointment. The staff is great! **MAP 12**

**Provenance Vineyards** - The Big Red Building - Wines: Sauv Blanc, Merlot, Cab Sauv, NV Port. 1695 St Helena Hwy (Hwy 29). St. Helena CA 94574 www.provenancevineyards.com (707) 968-3633 TF: $$-$$$ Hrs: 10-5:30

This is a big spacious winery that is making some seriously good wines. They have a nice gift section and social tasting room with an expansive tasting bar, a small gift area and a nice staff. **Map 19**

**Quintessa** - The Curving Wall - Wines: Bordeaux Blends. 1601 Silverado Trail Rutherford CA 94573 www.quintessa.com (707) 967-1601 TF: $$$ Hrs: by Appt.

This high end winery focuses on one Bordeaux-style blend that they offer with a food pairing. The tasting and tour is moderately expensive but the facility is beautiful. They are easy to spot of the Silverado Trail due to their remarkable building, built in a curve. The caves go directly into the hillside behind the building and the tasting room sits on top like a hat. They have a great staff and they are surrounded by their vineyards which are Biodynamic/Organic vineyards. Allow 1 -1/2 to 2 hours for the tour and tasting. **Map 19**

**Quixote Winery** - Most Unique Buildings - Wines: Cab Sauv, Grenache and Mourvèdre, Petite Syrah. 6126 Silverado Trail Napa CA 94558 www.quixotewinery.com (707) 944-2659, TF: $$$, Hrs: First Appt at 10, last 2:30.

This is one of Napa's most unique and intimate winery buildings. They do a great sit-down tasting. Allow 1 to 2 hours for the tour and tasting on Mon-Thurs. They are closed Wednesdays. They do tastings only on Friday and Saturday. Many people come here just to see the building, but the wines and hospitality are great too! **Map 17**

**Raymond Vineyard** & Cellar - Zinfandel Lane - Wines: Cab Sauv, Merlot, Chard, Sauv Blanc, Blends, Petite Sirah, Rosé, Meritage.  849 Zinfandel Ln. St. Helena  CA  94574  www.raymondvineyards.com  (707) 963-3141 TF: $$ - $$$  Hrs: 10-4  Appt.

This is owned by Jean Charles Boisett of Burgundy & Napa and he has transformed it into a show piece with diverse educational opportunities and delightful experiences. You have to see it for yourself, it is more than worth the time. The Raymond family is part of the Beringer family and was once involved in running that winery. **Map 19**

**Razi Winery** - Southern Silverado Trail  - Wines: Estate Chard plus other wines.  3106 Silverado Trail  Napa  CA  94558  (707) 224-4299  TF: $$ Hrs: Mon-Sat by Appt.

This is a newer, small, family run winery at the southern edge of the Silverado Trail. It is easy to spot their bright yellow sign. **Map 17**

**Reata** - Aka Jamieson Ranch Vineyards - Eastern Napa - Wines: A wide variety - 1 Kirkland Ranch Rd. Napa  www.ValleyGateVineyards.com  (707) 254-8673  TF: $$  Hrs: 10-5.

A large, rambling winery with a high ceilinged tasting room on the route from Hwy 80 to the Napa Valley, very popular with charter buses since they can handle the groups and the wines are moderately priced. **MAP 16**

**Regusci Winery** - Stags Leap District  - Wines: Cab Sauv, Merlot, Zin, and Chard.  5584 Silverado Trail  Napa  CA  94558  www.regusciwinery.com (707) 254-0403  TF: $$  Hrs: 10-5

Their stone barrel barn is the oldest winery building in the Stags Leap District. This is a friendly working farm, because the Regusci family manages vineyards for some very high-quality wineries. They sell grapes to others and lease some of their land out to other wineries. But they also make their own, and their wines come from the vineyards closest to the barn and tasting room. Every year their wines get better and better.  They have a great staff and a beautiful property and it is one of our favorite places to bring clients. They also have cute dogs, but please don't feed them. If you want to get the feeling of authentic Napa this is the place to come. For the high quality, the wines are a great deal. They carry some gifts and have a wonderful picnic area with lots of shade trees. They also make olive oil. **Map 17**

**Revana Family Vineyard** - Ultra Premium by Appointment - Wines: Cab Sauv, Merlot. 2930 St Helena Hwy (Hwy 29). N. St. Helena CA 94574 www.revanawine.com (707) 967-8814 TF: $$$ Hrs: 10-4 by Appt When Dr. Revana purchased the property, he put together a great team for this small ultra-premium winery, just off the road above St. Helena. Right next to it is the very beautifully designed tasting room. The wines are excellent and it is a sit-town tasting with a lot of style. The tasting is not overly long, so it fits in well with other appointments. **MAP 10**

**Reverie Vineyard & Winery** - Circle of Redwoods - Wines: Bordeaux varietals, Cab Franc, Cab Sauv, Sauv Blanc, Barbera, Rousanne. 1520 Diamond Mountain Rd. Calistoga CA 94515 www.reveriewine.com (707) 942-6800 TF: $$ Hrs: 10-5 by Appt
They are tucked at the end of a side road on Diamond Mountain, just a short distance from Route 29, before the road starts climbing. This is a great combination of rustic and elegant. The hillside vineyards surround the winery. The tasting begins in the cave and finishes in a fairy circle of Redwood Trees. They make complex and beautifully crafted wines. The staff is personable and knowledgeable. They have a very loyal customer base so they sometimes run out of wine, so call them first. **MAP 10**

**Reynolds Family Winery** - Southern Silverado - Wines: Cab Sauv, Pinot Noir, Chard, Persistence. 3266 Silverado Trail Napa CA 94558 www.reynoldsfamilywinery.com (707) 258-2558 TF: $$$ Hrs: 10:30-4:30 by appt.
It is a little surprising to find a winery that is this comfortable and relaxed, where the wines are so good, and it also very convenient from downtown Napa. It is a nice combination, and only their modest appearing entrance, right off of the Silverado Trail, keeps them from being overwhelmed with customers. They have a great side patio overlooking the pond, and they offer tours of the winery and vineyards. **Map 17**

**Robert Biale Vineyards** - Oak Knoll Zins - Wines: Zin, Petite Sirah, Barbera, and Sangiovese. 4038 Big Ranch Road Napa CA 94558 www.robertbialevineyards.com(707) 257-7555 TF: $ CWP Hrs: 10-5 instant Appt. This is another of those great Napa families that have growing good grapes for years. They make wonderful Zinfandels, and they offer them with that wonderful, relaxed Napa hospitality. They have an intimate, very pleasant tasting room with views of the vineyards, and a great staff that knows all of the great stories associated with the winery. **Map 17**

**Robert Keenan Winery** - Spring Mountain - Wines: Cab Sauv, Merlot, Zin, Syrah, Chard. 3660 Spring Mountain Rd. St. Helena CA 94574 www.keenanwinery.com (707) 963-9177 TF: $ Hrs: 11-4 by Appt
This is a very friendly winery about half the way up Spring Mountain.

The drive is a little narrow but pretty. They are often open to a last minute appointment and they make great wines. The site had a winery on it before Prohibition and the owners did a beautiful job of restoring the building and vineyards. **MAP 12**

**Robert Mondavi Winery** - A Gracious Estate - Wines: Fumé Blanc, Chard, Pinot Noir, Merlot, Cab Sauv, Moscato d'Oro, Dry Rosé.  7801 St Helena Hwy (Hwy 29).  Oakville  94558   www.robertmondaviwinery.com  (707) 968-2001   Hrs: 10-5  TF: $$ - $$$$$

Robert Mondavi was Napa's patron saint of marketing, a brilliant personality who was a tremendous influence on Napa's development. This big, Spanish style winery is almost a pilgrimage for many. It includes some of Napa's best land, midway up the valley with the mountains towering above the vineyards. The spacious, rambling winery features sculptures, gardens, a gift shop, multiple tours, and both a standard tasting room and the reserve "To Kalon" tasting room where the big Cabernet Sauvignon is poured. These are available both in flights and individually. The winery is now owned by Constellation Brands, but they have the same staff and the Mondavi family still owns numerous other wineries in the valley.  The winery is said to be on the less desirable western side of Hwy 29, the thinking being that it was easier to catch inbound visitors on the eastern side of the road, but clearly, Robert Mondavi overcame this perceived disadvantage. Francis Ford Coppola doesn't complain too much either.  **Map 19**

**Robert Sinskey Vineyards** - Stags Leap Biodynamic  - Wines: Bordeaux, Burgundy, Zin -  6320 Silverado Trail  Napa  CA  94558   www.robertsinskey.com  (707) 944-9090.  TF: $$ - $$$$$ w/ food pairings    Hrs: 10-4:30

This modern building sits above the road surrounded with lavender flowers and gardens on the Silverado Trail just south of Yountville Crossroad. When you enter the high vaulted space, you enjoy the aromas coming from the commercial kitchen in the back corner. One of the owners is a well known chef and cook book author and this winery has some of the best bar snacks in the valley. They have a delightful working garden that supplies the kitchen planted around the winery and a great patio with lots of seating. Their caves are behind the winery and are used for special events. They have a great collection of food related books and some nice gifts and they do some interesting wines. This is a fun place that draws a younger crowd. It is a Biodynamic/Organic winery.  **Map 17**

**Robinson Family Vineyards**  - Stags Leap District  - Wines: Cab Sauv, Merlot - 5880 Silverado Trail  Napa  CA  94558   www.robinsonfamilyvineyards.com (707) 944-8004  TF: $$  Hrs: by Appt

This is a small, family-run winery down a long country road that has few signs to mark it. You find it by looking for the street numbers. It is down a shared road/drive and then look for their small winery signs. The wines are very good. The family that makes them is great, the tasting room is small and relaxed and visiting there gives you a sense of authentic Napa.

They are by appointment but on the weekends a quick call should be enough warning. **Map 17**

**Rombauer Vineyards** - Hill Top Perch - Wines: Cab Sauv, Merlot, Chard, Zin, Port - 3522 Silverado Trail N. St. Helena CA 94574 www.rombauervineyards.com (707) 963-5170 TF: $$ Hrs: 10-5

Their winery is perched on its own hill, and it sits on a mile of narrow caves. Rombauer is a long time favorite, very well known in restaurants for their Chardonnay. The family developed the winery over many years while the father was an airline pilot and the mother managed another winery. They are part of the same family as the authors of the book 'The Joy of Cooking'. They sell the book, and if you visit the Culinary Institute of America, only a few minutes away, they have a display showing all of the editions from the first, very small and simple book. Rombauer makes very appealing wines, they have a friendly staff, a great picnic area, wonderful views and aviation memorabilia. In season on the weekends, they employ a valet service to manage the cars because they have limited parking and lots of visitors. They also do wonderful tours. **MAP 10**

**Round Pond Estate** - Rutherford Dust and Olives - Wines: Cab Sauv, Nebbiolo and then some. 875 Rutherford Rd. Rutherford CA 94573 www. roundpond.com (707) 302-2575 TF: $$$ Hrs: 11-4 by Appt Thu-Mon

This family owns hundreds of acres of vines in Rutherford, although most of the grapes are sold to other wineries. They also grow olives and their well known press is across the way. They do olive tastings there by appointment. The rather spectacular winery at the end of a long palm tree lined drive was created for the small percentage of grapes that they hold to for their own tasting room. It only figures that they hold onto some of the best. The tasting room is beautiful and elegant, the staff is knowledgeable and the only hard part is getting an appointment, since they make limited wines and are only open on certain days. However, it is worth the effort because this is one of Rutherford's great wine estates. **MAP 18**

**Rubicon Estate** - See Inglenook **Map 19**

**Rudd** - Very private and Beautiful - Wines: Cab Sauv, Chard, Sauv, Blanc, Blends. 500 Oakville Cross Rd. Oakville CA 94562 www.ruddwines.com (707) 944-8577 TF: $$$$, Hrs: Tue-Sat by Appt

This is a winery for the collector. It is owned by Leslie Rudd, the owner of Dean and DeLuca and the Oakville Grocery and it is quite a showplace. The tasting is expensive and so are the wines, but for the serious enthusiast it is a great experience. The gardens are lovely, and the winery is state of the art, although the tasting is normally limited to the main building, there are extensive caves on the property. The gardens are beautiful and it is quite a show place. The tours are at 10:00, and they handle a maximum of 8 guests. There is a "Request for Visit Form" on the website that you fax in. Wines: Cabernet Sauvignon, Chardonnay, Sauvignon, Blanc, Blends. **Map 19**

**Rustridge Winery** - Chiles Valley - Wines: Bordeaux and Burgundy. 2910 Lower Chiles Valley Road, St. Helena CA 94574  www.rustridge.com (707) 965-9353  TF: $  Hrs: 10-4

It is a 25 minute ride from the valley floor to this far end of Chiles Valley (rhymes with miles). Back in the 1950's this was a horse ranch, and while there are still horses on the property, the main business is the winery and the Rustridge Bed & Breakfast, a rustic but charming place to stay in the hills above Napa. They are open without an appointment, although the distance and the route down little country roads makes a casual drop pretty rare. But if you like to take a beautiful drive and sample their excellent wines, then plan on the time. Out in that same area is the Nichelini winery.  **MAP 20**

**Rutherford Grove Winery** & Vineyards - Small Family Winery  - Wines: Cab Sauv, Merlot, Sauv Blanc, Petite Sirah, Sangiovese.  1673 Highway 29 Rutherford CA 94573  www.rutherfordgrove.com  (707) 963-0544  TF: $$,  Hrs: 10-4:30. This family first arrived in Napa in the late 1800's. All of their wines are from estate grapes and they own vineyards in both Napa and Lake County. It is a family winery with a great staff, good wines, a friendly atmosphere and a convenient location nearby Provenance, Franciscan, Alpha Omega, Sullivan and Fleury. They have picnic tables and some interesting features in the tasting room. Their most popular wine is their Sauvignon Blanc. The winery is surrounded by their vineyards. **Map 19**

**Rutherford Hill Winery** - Great Views and Tour  - Wines: Zin Port, Merlot, Cab Sauv, Cab Franc, Sangiovese, Blends, Petite Verdot, Chard, Syrah, Malbec, Sauv Blanc. 200 Rutherford Hill Rd.  Rutherford CA 94558  www. rutherfordhill.com(707) 963-1871  TF: $$ - $$$  Hrs: 10-5

They are located on a hillside overlooking the valley with great views. This is a fun winery with good wines and they do an excellent tour. It is owned by the Terlato family, who also owns Chimney Rock, and is a major wine distributor. They are one of the product sponsors of the popular show 'Top Chef'. You can picnic at tables under hundred year old olive trees with views of the valley below for a small fee. When the property was first developed, they discovered the grove of olive trees, but had no idea who had planted them. The owner's wife made it her mission to restore the grove. They have nice indoor and outdoor tasting areas that can accommodate groups. They do their tours,

Saturdays from 11:30-3:30 on the half hour, Weekdays 11:30-1:30-3:30. It includes a tasting. Call ahead with groups. **Map 19**

**Rutherford Ranch** - Several Labels - Wines: Cab Sauv, Chard, Merlot, Sauv Blanc, Zin, White Zin, Port, Muscato. 1680 Silverado Trail St. Helena CA 94574 www.rutherfordranch.com (707) 967-5120 TF: $$ Hrs: 10-4:30

There are three wineries that start with 'Rutherford'. This is the most unusual because it serves almost like a collective tasting room. Various labels are tasted here including Round Hill. It sits directly opposite Conn Creek Road and across the street from the Conn Creek Winery. On the hills above is the hotel Auberge du Soleil. **Map 19**

**Saddleback Cellars** - Rustic in a Great Location - Wines: Pinot Blanc, Pinot Grigio, Chard, Viognier, Merlot, Old Vine Zin, Cab Sauv. 7802 Money Rd. Oakville CA 94562 www.saddlebackcellars.com (707) 944-1305 TF: $$ Hrs: 10-4 instant Appt. The winery is owned by Nils Venge, a very-respected consulting winemaker. It is a small winery on Money Road which is across from the entrance to Silver Oak Winery. Tastings are done outside on picnic tables next to the vines. The wines are very good and they are convenient to a number of other great wineries. It is surprising to find such a relaxed, natural winery tucked among all of the heavy hitters of Oakville. **MAP 9**

**Saintsbury Vineyard** - Carneros - Wines: Pinot Noir, Syrah, Chard. 1500 Los Carneros Ave. Napa www.saintsbury.com (707) 252-0592 TF: $, Hrs: Mon-Fri by Appt.

This winery is respected for their Pinot Noir. They are open by appointment during the week, and it is just a short distance off of the main road, although they are not clearly marked. You have to depend on the street signs and mailbox numbers. They have good distribution, so they do not focus on tastings, but if you are an enthusiast, call them. **MAP 15**

**Salvestrin Vineyard** & Winery - With a Bed and Breakfast - Wines: Cab Sauv, Sangiovese, Retaggio (Red Blend), Sauv Blanc, Petite Sirah. 397 Main St. St. Helena CA 94574 www.salvestrinwinery.com (707) 963-5105 TF: $$$-$$$$$ Hrs: by Appt. This winery close to downtown St. Helena. The tastings are private in the small second story tasting room with nice views of the vineyards. They have been farming Napa since 1932 and released their first vintage in 1994. The wines are very good, the winemaking facility is very modern and the experience is enjoyable. **MAP 23**

**Schramsberg Vineyards** - Classic Sparklers - Wines: Sparkling Wines and Cab Sauv - 1400 Schramsberg Rd. Calistoga CA 94515 www.schramsberg. com (707) 942-4558 TF: $$$$ with tour Hrs: 10-4 by Appt.

This is a historic winery at the top of a long, winding road. Allow extra travel time and arrive early to enjoy the newly expanded hospitality center.

The tasting includes the tour and they are set up at specific times, so you don't want to be late. When Robert Louis Stevenson honeymooned in Napa, he visited Jacob Schram and enjoyed his wine. After years of abandonment, the Davies family purchased the property and restored it beautifully, producing world class sparkling wines in the process. **MAP 10**

**Schweiger Vineyards** - Top of Spring Mountain  - Wines: Sauv Blanc, Chard, Merlot, Cab Sauv, Petite Sirah, Port.   4015 Spring Mountain Rd.  St. Helena  CA  94574  www.schweigervineyards.com  (707) 963-4882   TF: $$  Hrs: 11-4 by Appt. This family-run winery is in a beautiful location at the top of Spring Mountain. They have great views and sometimes start the tasting upstairs on the lawn, but the main tasting is done in the barrel room. Even though the wineries on Spring Mountain are all by appointment, including Schweiger, and they have a gate to ensure that, they are often open to last-minute appointments. The father grows the grapes, the son makes them into wine, and the daughter runs the tasting room. How cool is that?  **MAP 12**

**Seavey Vineyard** - Conn Valley  - Wines: Cab Sauv, Merlot.
1310 Conn Valley Rd. St. Helena  94574   www.seaveyvineyard.com   (707) 963-8339 TF: $$   Hrs: 10-4 by Appt
It is a fifteen minute drive out Conn Valley to the winery. The stone dairy barn that now serves as the winery was built in 1881. The hillsides are planted with grapes. It is a beautiful place, a nice tasting and very good wines. **MAP 13**

**Sequoia Grove Winery** - Relaxed and Friendly  - Wines: Cab Sauv, Chard, Syrah. 8338 St Helena Hwy (Hwy 29). S. Rutherford CA  94558   www.sequoiagrove.com   (707) 944-2945,  TF: $$ - $$$,  Hrs: 10:30-5
They are next to some of the area's most famous wineries and they can hold their own for quality. They have a charming, relaxed tasting room and a friendly staff. They do sit down chocolate, cheese & wine pairings by appointment. Look for the Sequoia trees as your landmark.  **Map 19**

**Shafer Vineyards** - Ultra Premium Stags Leap District Producer  - Wines: Chard, Cabernet, Blends.   6154 Silverado Trail  Napa CA 94558  www.shafervineyards.com  (707) 944-2877   TF: $$$$   Hrs: Tastings at 10am & 2pm Mon-Fri by Appt
They are a family-owned and run winery. Their Hillside Select is a world famous wine that comes from the beautiful canyon that you drive through on the way to the winery. As you drive north on Silverado Trail they are on the right side. There is no sign, just a number. They expanded their hospitality center and it is spacious and light-filled. They are one of Napa's great ultra-premium producers and a wonderful family. In a recent competition between the best of Italy and the USA, their wine won top honors. Their tastings are by appointment and take place sitting down in a lovely conference

room with glass walls that look out over the vineyards. The tasting is admittedly expensive but worth it for the enthusiast. Plan ahead when making your appointment since they have a limited number of slots. **Map 17**

**Sherwin Family Vineyards** - Great Building on Spring Mountain - Wines: Cab Sauv, Blends.  4060 Spring Mountain Rd. St. Helena CA 94574  www.sherwinfamilyvineyards.com    (707) 963-1154    TF: $ - $$$$   Hrs: by Appt

They taste in a great building looking out at the vineyards. It feels like visiting a friend's home for a tasting. Their Cabernet blend gets consistently high marks. Since it is on Spring Mountain, and by appointment, we suggest that you allow extra time to get there. It is a minimum of 20 minutes from Hwy 29 in St. Helena to the top of Spring Mountain, and then Sherwin Family is on a little extension where going slow is normal. Navigation Tip: They are located on the top of Spring Mountain. Take the road up the hill until you are on the top. After you pass the Schweiger winery on the right, look for a road going to the right and a large number of mail boxes. There will also be winery signs. Turn right there and follow the signs for the number, 4060 and the winery name. This is the same drive that goes to Barnett Winery. **MAP 12**

**Signorello Vineyards** - Hillside Perch  - Wines: Cab Sauv, Zin, Pinot Noir, Syrah, Sauv-Semillon Blend.  4500 Silverado Trail  Napa  CA  94558  www.signorellovineyards.com    (707) 255-5990  TF: $  Hrs: 10:30-5

This is a charming, small family winery perched on the hillsides of Silverado just north of Darioush. They produce well-made wines from estate vineyards. They make a Sauvignon Blanc, Semillon blend, because their winemaker, Pierre Birebent is French and that's the traditional blend. Pierre is rare in Napa because he's both the vineyard manager and winemaker, and all of their grapes come from within walking distance from the winery. So he guides the grapes from the fields into the bottles. **Map 17**

**Silenus Vintners** - Collective Winery Oak Knoll   5225 Solano Ave.  Napa CA 94558    www.silenusvintners.com    (707) 299-3930  TF: $$ - $$$  Hrs: 10-4:30 by Appt, instant

This is a very pleasant tasting room that represents the wineries that use this facility. They have both a bar and a beautiful conference room. It is very convenient to downtown Napa, nearby Laird, and Elyse. **Map 17**

**Silver Oak Cellars** - Big Popular Red Wines  - Wines: Cab Sauv Blends.  915 Oakville Cross Rd.  Oakville 94558   www.silveroak.com   (707) 944-8808  Hrs: 9-5 (winter to 4)   TF: $$$

Several years ago, Silver Oak suffered a flood followed by a fire. Before the locusts could show up the owners bulldozed the site (except for their signature water tower) and built a new, bigger winery, faced with antique blocks from an 1800's flour mill. It's great!  The tasting room is spacious, the parking easy, and the buildings are easily seen from the Oakville Crossroad at the end of its long, tree-lined driveway. The primary wine is a big Cabernet blend, in two versions, one from Napa and the other from Sonoma's Alexander Valley. Silver Oak sits in the center of the Napa Valley on the flattest part so the views of vineyards, hills and valley are unobstructed. The grounds and seating around the fountain are lovely. They're well known for their commitment to using American oak barrels, which gives the wine a stronger vanilla flavor. This decision has served them well as the strength of the Euro has seen the price of the French barrels many wineries use go through the roof. **Map 19**

**Silverado Vineyards** - Great Views in Stags Leap  - Wines: Sauv Blanc, Chard, Merlot, Sangiovese, Cab Sauv.  6121 Silverado Trail  Napa 94558  www.silveradovineyards.com   (707) 257-1770  TF: $$ - $$$   Hrs: 10:30-5

For a large winery, Silverado is remarkably romantic. It might be the Spanish-style building, the location perched on a hill in the Stags Leap district, the gorgeous views over the vineyards from the patio, or the comfortable tasting room. The wines are very well made and reasonably priced. The staff is friendly and accustomed to visitors from all over the world. The drive up to the top of their hill seems steeper than it really is, but the convex mirrors that allow you to see around the corners are very helpful. They have nice gift shop with an abundance of interesting books. Take some time to sit out on the patio with a glass of wine and enjoy the view and bring your camera There is something very special about this place, with its collection of small, rounded hills that gather in the morning fog and hold it there as the Sun rises and sends rainbows through the vines. The winery is owned by Walt Disney's daughter so maybe some of the family magic rubbed off on the winery. **Map 17**

**Smith-Madrone**  - Spring Mountain Riesling  - Wines: Cab Sauv, Chard, Riesling.  4022 Spring Mountain Rd.  St. Helena CA 94574  www.smith-madrone.com  (707) 963-2283  TF: PIE     Hrs: Mon-Sat by Appt .

This is one of the earliest of the new wineries on the mountain having their first commercial vintage in 1977. They are very down home and relaxed, with great views, cool caves, nice folk and the mountains best and most famous Riesling. They do small production and are by appointment. **MAP 12**

**Sodaro Estate Winery** & Vineyard - Eastern Napa  - Wines: Cab Sauv, Cab Franc, Blends.  24 Blue Oak Lane  Napa  CA  94558  www.sodarowines.com  (707) 975-6689  TF: $$$ CWP  Hrs: by Appt

This charming family winery on the east side of Napa is newly opened for appointments. They have a great vineyard and winemaking team and the vineyards in that part of Napa have been producing excellent results so we expect great things here.  **MAP 6**

**Spottswoode Winery** - Central Saint Helena   - Wines: Cab Sauv, Sauv Blanc, Blends.   1902 Madrona Ave. St. Helena  CA  94574   www.spottswoode.com    (707) 963-0134 TF: $ - $$$    Hrs: 10am Tue & Fri by Appt

    This is truly a family winery located in downtown St. Helena. The owner and winemaking team are almost all women and they specialize in Sauvignon Blanc and Cabernet Sauvignon. Their permit allows them very limited visitors so book 6–8 weeks in advance for an appointment. This property has a lot of history, including their ghost winery from the 1800's, and the estate house and gardens, which are beautifully planted are part of the tour. They do very small production. **MAP 23**

**Spring Mountain Vineyards** - Classic  Spring Mountain   - Wines: Syrah, Cab Sauv, Sauv Blanc. 2805 Spring Mountain Rd. St. Helena  CA  94574   www.springmtn.com  (707) 967-4188  TF: $$$ with tour    Hrs: 10-5 by Appt

    This is a grand estate that has their wineries and mansion at the foot of Spring Mountain, and their vineyards stretching up on the hillsides above them. They are one of the biggest vineyards on Spring Mountain, being a combination of several large properties. They make seriously wonderful wines. The mansion and gardens are remarkable and were used in the television series Falcon Crest. They have a good staff, with a lot of style. You should allow two hours for the tour that includes the caves, winery and a sit down tasting in the mansion. The tasting fees are applied to your purchase. **MAP 12**

**St. Clement Vineyards** - Great Views and Picnics  - Wines: Cab Sauv, Merlot, Sauv Blanc, Chard, Syrah.  2867 N. St Helena Hwy (Hwy 29). St. Helena  CA  94574   www.stclement.com    (800) 331-8266  TF: $$ - $$$    Hrs: 10-4

    This Victorian tasting room overlooking Hwy 29 was built as a home in the late 1800's. It served as a winery, then a home again and is now back to being a winery. It is owned by Beringer. They have a cute gifts and great views from their patios. They also have wonderful picnic tables on several levels. The tasting bar is small but the room is nice. They often have Panama hats for sale which are helpful on our sunny Napa days. The very modern winery is at the back of the property. The wines are quite good! **MAP 10**

**St. Supéry Vineyards** - Understated Elegance  - Wines: Sauv Blanc, Cab Sauv, Merlot, Chard, Unoaked Chard, Syrah, Cab Franc.  8440 St Helena Hwy (Hwy 29). Rutherford  CA  94558  www.stsupery.com  (707) 963-4507  TF: $$-$$$  Hrs: 10-5

    They are owned by a French winery family and fronted by a beautiful Victorian house, but the tasting room and winery is in a modern structure. They have a very spacious, well lit main tasting room and nice gift shop. On the second floor is a gallery, a self-tour and the reserve tasting room, which is by appointment. They make good, European-style wines, complex and satisfying. Many of the grapes are sourced from Pope Valley.  For the best tasting spot, find a place at the bar away from the entrance. If you are coming with a group of seven or more, or a limousine, you need to call ahead. **Map 19**

**Staglin Family Vineyard** - By Limited Appointment  - Wines: Chard, Cab Sauv, Sangiovese.   1570 Bella Oaks Ln.  Rutherford  CA  94573  www.staglin-family.com   (707) 963-3994  TF: $$$$   Hrs: 11-3 Mon-Fri by Appt

This is a well-respected family-run winery with stellar wines that is known for their architecture and their organic methods. They have a great cave complex and do their tastings by appointment. They have a very pleasant and knowledgeable staff. **Map 19**

**Stag's Leap Wine Cellars** - Judgment of Paris Winner  - Wines: Sauv Blanc, Chard, Merlot, Cab Sauv.  5766 Silverado Trail  Napa  94558  www. cask23.com   (707) 261-6441   TF: $$ - $$$$   Hrs: 10-4:30

The Stags Leap district is in the southeastern corner of the Napa Valley. It's also the name of two wineries separated by an apostrophe. Stag's Leap Wine Cellars is one of Napa's most famous wineries, yet surprisingly low key, tucked at the bottom of a hill off the Silverado Trail. A stairway brings you to the tasting/tank room. Even though it became famous by winning top honors for its Cabernet blend at the 1976 Judgment of Paris tasting, the tasting room seems like an afterthought. There are two small tasting bars, standard to the left, reserve to the right. Unseen by the general public but available on arranged tours are wonderful caves with a banquet table and some unique features. If you love BIG RED Napa wines then you should come here, but don't expect a spectacular tasting, the staff is as low-keyed as the environment. The original family sold it in 2008 to Antinori and Chateau St Michele. **Map 17**

**Stags' Leap Winery** - By Appointment Petite Syrah   - Wines: Viognier, Chard, Merlot, Cab Sauv, Petite Syrah.   6150 Silverado Trail  Napa CA  94558 www.stagsleapwinery.com   (707) 944-1303    TF: $$$$ includes tour     Hrs: by Appt.  This winery has tons of history and stories back to the 1800's.  They taste in the Ivy covered Manor House, which has been featured in both television and movies and it is not an easy appointment to set up, so plan on making your plans 8 weeks in advance. Because of the similarity of their name with their neighbors, Stag's Leap Wine Cellars, there was an extended lawsuit that resulted in the placement of an apostrophe to differentiate the two. When their neighbor won the Judgment of Paris for their Cabernet, their reputation was enhanced by association. However, their approach is much different, and they are most known for their less traditional wines, especially their fantastic Petite Syrah. It is currently owned by Beringer.  **Map 17**
**Steltzner Vineyards** - Site bought by Odette **Map 17**

**Sterling Vineyards** - Ride the Gondola to Wine & Views  - Wines: Cab Sauv, Merlot, Chard, Pinot Noir, Shiraz, Sauv Blanc, Blends.  1111 Dunaweal Ln. Calistoga 94515   www.sterlingvineyards.com   (707) 942-3344   TF: $$$   Hrs: 10-4:30.   This iconic winery outside downtown Calistoga is one of Napa's most visited, famous for the aerial tramway that brings you to the mountain top tasting room. They were the first winery to charge for tastings many years ago and the tramway was their excuse. This is a big brand and they also bring grapes in from outside of Napa to supplement their product line, but it is a fun time, with great views, a good gift shop and a wide variety of wines. They do both standard and reserve tastings. Plan on some time for waiting in line and riding the tramway so allow at least two hours for your visit. As you travel north and pass Larkmead Lane you can see Sterling's bright white building perched on its hilltop in the middle of the valley. Check on line for coupons for discounted admission tickets. **MAP 10**

**Stony Hill Vineyard** - Tucked Away - Wines: Chard, All White Wines. 3331 N. St Helena Hwy (Hwy 29) St. Helena CA 94574   www.stonyhillvineyard.com   (707) 963-2636   TF: $   Hrs: 9-5 Mon-Fri by Appt

This is a small winery up a long narrow road. Saying that it is on Hwy 29 is not quite accurate. You enter via the drive to the Bale Grist Mill and then just before the park's entrance you take the drive to the left which goes to the winery. They are very nice people who make good wine in an interesting location. The tasting includes a tour and it may be a bit of ride but it is well worth the time. **MAP 10**

**Storybook Mountain Winery** - The Northern Edge  - Wines: Zin, Cab Sauv, Blends. 3835 Highway 128  Calistoga CA 94515  www.storybookwines.com  (707) 942-5310 TF: $  8 or more $$   Hrs: Mon-Sat by appt.

This is a beautiful location on the edge between the Napa Valley and Knight's Valley. The tour and tasting is by appointment, and normally done by the owner. It is a very special place, although a bit of a ride. The tasting is done in the caverns.   **MAP 10**

**Sullivan Vineyards Winery** - A Rambling Family Winery  - Wines: Rosé, Chard, Bordeaux Blend, Cab Sauv, Merlot.   1090 Galleron Rd.   St. Helena CA 94574  www.sullivanwine.com  (877) 244-7337   TF: $$- $$$$   Hrs: 10-5 by Appt.  They make big red wines and create a gracious tasting experience at their property behind the Franciscan Winery. The sign is on Galleron road and leads you down a long  driveway. The tasting room is simple  with a bar and conference table, but the outside patio is delightful. Off in the distance is a pond with a fountain. The other winery building, complete with patios and event spaces faces the tasting room. **Map 19**

**Summers Estate Wines** - Calistoga Friendly - Wines: Cab Sauv, Chard, Merlot, Charbono, Zin, Muscat Canelli, Petite Sirah.   1171 Tubbs Ln. Calistoga CA 94515  www.sumwines.com   (707) 942-5508     TF: $$, Hrs: 10:30

- 4:30. This family winery sources their own grapes from nearby vineyards and makes good wines at a reasonable price. The tasting room is sunny and friendly, the tasting is relaxed and informative. The winery is very true to its location, with that relaxed, gracious style that is typical of Calistoga. They also have a nice gift section and picnic tables. They are just across the street from Envy Wines. **MAP 10**

**Summit Lake Vineyards** & Winery - Howell Mountain - Wines: Cab Sauv, Zin, Zin Port. 2000 Summit Lake Dr. Angwin CA 94508 www.summit-lakevineyards.com (707) 965-2488 TF: $$ Hrs: by Appt.

This is a small family winery about 20 minutes from the Silverado Trail. The tasting is at the home of the owners and outside in the garden if weather permits. Their first commercial vintage was in 1978 and won gold medals. They do very small production on site, and some wines are only available at the winery. For the quality, the prices are very good. **MAP 13**

**Sutter Home Winery** - Big Selling Brand - Wines: Variety of modestly priced wines - 277 St Helena Hwy S(Hwy 29). St. Helena 94574 www.sutterhome.com (707) 963-3104 TF: $ Hrs: 10-5

This is one of Napa's biggest wineries, yet most of the grapes are brought in from other areas. They are known for their White Zinfandel, one of the biggest selling wines in America. The owners, the Trinchero family, own numerous wineries in Napa. It is a big, spacious tasting room with a friendly staff, a wide variety of wines and a nice gift shop. The tastings are complimentary and the price point is modest. Many of their Zinfandel grapes come from Amador County, many miles to the east in the Sierra Madre foothills. This was gold-rush country and viticulture was started there by miners who this as a good alternative to panning for gold. Their Amador county, deep red Zinfandel is their stand-out wine and a good deal. White Zinfandel is miss-named, being a pink wine, the reason being that the original wine was dry and white. It started off as a 'throw away juice', drawn off before fermentation so that the remainder would make a deeper, richer Zinfandel. One year they got sloppy and left some skins in the juice, and then the fermentation got stuck leaving some residual sugar. This pink, sweet accident was 'White Zinfandel'. They were stuck with the name and it's been a big seller ever since. **Map 19**

**Swanson Vineyards & Winery** - Prettiest Tasting Room Ever - Wines: Merlot, Pinot Grigio, Rosato, Petite Sirah, Sangiovese, Syrah, Chard, Blends, Muscat. 1271 Manley Ln. Rutherford CA 94573 www.swansonvineyards.com. (707) 944-1642 TF: $$$, Hrs: by Appt

These are great wines poured in an elegant tasting room, often with a food-pairing. The interior of the tasting room is delightful. This is the family that created Swanson Frozen dinners. It is not surprising how many families that made their fortune in food go on to open wineries. Wine is food too, after

,all! They are by appointment and you are given a specific time to arrive. The gate opens automatically five minutes before the appointment. They do wonderful special events. **Map 19**

**Tamber Bey** - New Facility with Horses - Wines: Bordeaux, Burgundy - 1251 Tubbs Ln, Calistoga, CA 94515 - www.tamberbey.com - (707) 942-2100 - TF: $$$-$$$$ - Hrs: 10-6 The vineyards are in Yountville and this facility incldes a large stable. **MAP 23**

**Terra Valentine** - Spring Mountain Exotic - Wines: Pinot Noir, Cab Sauv, Bordeaux. 3787 Spring Mountain Rd. St. Helena CA 94574 www.terravalentine.com (707) 967-8340 TF: $$$ CWP Hrs: by Appt

This is an extraordinary building with a story that is worth the ride by itself. This is a fun tasting with a group of friends or family, but plan to spend a couple of hours here. The wines are quite good and the place is memorable. They are half way up Spring Mountain on the left side and easy to find, with a nice, wide driveway. **MAP 12**

**The Terraces** - Adventurous - Wines: Zin, Cab Sauv, Balsamic vinegar. 1450 Silverado Trail, Rutherford CA 94574 www.terraceswine.com (707) 963-1707 TF: PIE 1 case Hrs: 10-4:30 Thu-Sun by Appt

They do their tour of this beautiful property in a 4-wheel drive that carries a maximum of five people; that is how many fit in the SUV. They have some of the few Zinfandel vines left in that section of Napa. At one time, the area was dominated by Zinfandel vines and Plum trees, but Cabernet Sauvignon has supplanted most of that. Fortunately, it didn't chase out their vines because their Zinfandel is great. They also make Balsamic vinegar. **Map 19**

**Trefethen Vineyards & Winery** - Historic Winery - Wines: Dry Riesling, Viognier, Chard, Pinot Noir, Cab Franc, Merlot, Cab Sauv, Late Harvest Riesling - 1160 Oak Knoll Ave. Napa CA 94558 www.trefethen.com (707) 255-7700 TF: $$ - $$$, Hrs: 10-4:30

They are located in an historic restored, wooden gravity fed winery from the 1800's with a great patio and cork oaks. The tasting room is visually connected to the barrel room by a glass wall. The tasting room is spacious and fun and they make estate wines of very high quality, but properly priced. There are so many reasons to visit Trefethen, including an outstanding Riesling, a grape which is produced by very few Napa wineries. They are one of the first wineries you come to on the right traveling up valley on Hwy 29. Navigation Tip: As you come north on Hwy 29, you turn right at the light at Oak Knoll Ave. The entrance to the winery will be on the left. If you want to continue north on the Silverado Trail, when you come out from the winery turn left, then left at the stop sign and immediately right. That will bring you over Oak Knoll Avenue to the Silverado Trail. Turning left there will bring you north through the Stags Leap district.  **Map 17**

**Tres Sabores** - Very Small by Appointment   - Wines: Zin, Cab Sauv, Petite Sirah, Petite Verdot, Sauv Blanc.     1620 S. Whitehall Ln.  St. Helena  CA 94574  www.tressabores.com   (707) 967-8027  TF: PIE  Hrs: by Appt.

This is a charming, small family winery on prime bench land with old vine Zinfandel and Cabernet Sauvignon vines. In nice weather, the tasting is done with the owner/winemaker outside at a picnic table, under huge olive trees. In cool weather, the tasting is done in the winery or at the owner's house. The hillsides are planted with grapes and pomegranates. Watch for the sheep in the vineyards as you arrive. This is hands-on winemaking so if you can, visit here during crush.  **Map 19**

**Trinchero Napa Valley** - Wine and Food   - Wines: Cab Sauv, Meritage, Sauv Blanc, Merlot, Petit Verdot.   3070 St Helena Hwy (Hwy 29).  St. Helena CA  94574   www.trincherowinery.com   (707) 963-3104   TF: $$   Hrs: 10-5

This is a destination hospitality center just north of downtown St. Helena, showcasing their best wines. Besides being a state of the art winery, it is also a state of the art culinary center. They are committed to expanding the enjoyment of food and wine. The winemaking team here is great and the wines are high quality and a good value. The Trinchero family owns numerous wineries and thousands of acres of vineyards throughout California, including Sutter Home.  **MAP 10**

**Trinitas Cellars** - Inside the Meritage Resort  - Wines: Chard, Pinot Noir, Pinot Blanc, Sauv Blanc, Mataro, Petit Sirah, Zin, Blends.     875 Bordeaux Way  Napa CA  94558  www.trinitascellars.com   (707) 251-1956, TF: $$ CWP  Hrs: 12 -8    *Second Lcation - 851 Napa Valley Corporate Way Ste. A Napa  CA  94558

One tasting room is inside the Meritage Resort in southern Napa. The grapes are sourced from far and wide and include a remarkable number of old vine wines, including Mataro, a rarely seen grape. The reserve tasting room is at the second address and by appointment.  **MAPs 21 & 16**

**Truchard Vineyard** - Carneros Gem  - Wines: Chard, Roussanne, Pinot Noir, Syrah, Zin, Merlot, Cab Franc, Cab Sauv, Petit Verdot, Tempranillo, Olive Oil. 3234 Old Sonoma Rd.  Napa  CA  94559   www.truChardvineyards.com  (707) 253-7153  TF: $$   Hrs: by Appt

The Truchard family makes wonderful wines, complex, delicious and interesting, at their property in the hills of Carneros. They are open by appointment and it is not always the easiest tasting to arrange, because they are a busy winery with a large customer list, but it is worth the effort. They've owned the land since 1974 and started making their own wines in 1989. They make a dozen wines including a Roussanne, which is unusual, and a Cabernet Sauvignon, which is rare in Carneros, an area generally considered too cool for this heat loving grape. The tasting room is basic, the caves are nice, dug into the hillside beneath the vineyards, and the hospitality is genuine. **MAP 15**

**Tudal Family Winery** - Homey and Relaxed  - Wines: Cab Sauv, Sauv Blanc. 1015 Big Tree Rd.  St. Helena CA  94574  www.tudalwinery.com (707) 484-3413  TF: $  Hrs: by Appt

This is a small, eccentric family-run winery that started in 1974, that produces very good wines at surprisingly reasonable prices. The property is filled with bits and pieces of their farming and winemaking history. These are nice people in a pretty part of the valley, just across the way from the Benessere Winery. **MAP 10**

**Tulocay Winery** - Eastern Napa - Wines: Pinot Noir, Cab Sauv, Merlot, Syrah, Zin, Chard. 1426 Coombsville Rd Napa.  www.TulocayWinery.com (707) 255-4064 TF: $  Hrs: By Appt  **MAP 6**

**Turnbull Wine Cellars** - Photo Gallery  - Wines: Sauv Blanc, Old Bull Red, Viognier, Toroso, Cab Sauv, Merlot, Barbera, Syrah.   8210 St Helena Hwy (Hwy 29).  Oakville CA  94562  www.turnbullwines.com  (707) 963-5839 TF: $$ - $$$  Hrs: 10-4:30

The original owner, William Turnbull, was the architect who built the Cakebread winery next door. Afterwards he built his own winery using similar materials and design. You can see other designs by him around the valley, including the neat buildings at Long Meadow Ranch. The current owner is a photographic art collector and the barrel room doubles as an art gallery. They have a nice tasting room and grounds, good wines and a great staff. **Map 19**

**Twomey Cellars** - Merlot Focus - Wines: Merlot, Pinot Noir, Sauv Blanc. 1183 Dunaweal Ln.  Calistoga CA  94515  www.twomeycellars.com  (707) 942-2489    TF:$$  Hrs: 9-4.  This winery is part of the same family as Silver Oak. They created this winery to specialize in Merlot based wines, which they do quite well. It has a spacious tasting room with windows into the barrel room. It is easy to find, being on the corner of Hwy 29 and Dunaweal Lane. It is located next door to Clo Pegase, Sterling Vineyards, and up the road from Castello di Amorosa, so it often gets overlooked in light of these big, destination wineries. There is a second Twomey winery in northern Sonoma that specializes in Pinot Noir. **MAP 10**

**V. Madrone** - Small with Lots of History  - Wines: Chard, Cab Sauv, Petite Sirah, Zin.  3199 St. Helena Highway N. St. Helena  CA  94574  www.vmadrone.com    (877) 994-6311  TF: Varies  PIE  Hrs: by Appt

They have only very recently opened to the public after a major rescue of the site and its buildings. This is a charming winery with great wines, a little north of downtown St. Helena. The property has an interesting history and the owners do the tastings and tell the story. **MAP 10**

**V. Sattui Winery** - The Best Deli - Wines: A very wide selection. 1111 White Ln. St. Helena 94574 www.vsattui.com (707) 963-7774 TF: $ - $$ Hrs: 9-6 9-5 in Winter

This winery proves that if you combine food, wine and shopping you are going to need more parking and they could use some. This is said to be Napa's busiest winery in part because it is home to the Valley's only winery deli, that is surrounded by picnic tables, a packed gift shop and a busy tasting room. They are centrally located on the northbound side of Route 29. The wines are average but they sell a lot. The tasting fee is modest, with standard and reserve tasting rooms, and the property is pretty, although crowded on the weekends. It was started in the 1970's by an entrepreneur whose family made wine in the late 1800's in San Francisco. He also owns Castello di Amorosa, the Tuscan style destination castle winery in Calistoga. If you like a bit of chaos, V. Sattui is a great place to do a tasting and eat lunch, but you can only eat food purchased there on the property. **Map 19**

**Van Der Heyden Vineyards** - Southern Silverado - Wines: Cab Sauv, Merlot, Chard. 4057 Silverado Trail Napa CA 94558 www.vanderheydenvineyards.com (707) 257-0130 TF: $$ Hrs: 10-6 . This is a small, rustic winery that sits at the southern end of the Silverado Trail across from the Soda Canyon Market. It is unique and friendly and worth a visit. The tasting is essentially outdoors. They make some good wine. **Map 17**

**Vermeil Wines/OnThEdge Winery** - Downtown Calistoga - Wines: Sauv Blanc, Charbono, Cab Franc, Cab Sauv, Zin. 1255 Lincoln Ave. Calistoga CA 94515 www.vermeilwines.com (707) 341-3054 TF: $ Hrs: 10-5:30-ish Sun-Thu 10-8-ish Fri-Sat

This tasting room is in downtown Calistoga. Their shaded tasting patio overlooks the Napa River and that makes it a perfect place for a picnic. The Vermeil name comes from the Super Bowl winning Football Coach, Dick Vermeil, a Calistoga native. (Yes, that Vermiel!) You can taste both the Vermeil and OnThEdge labels here in a spacious tasting room that is bright and conveniently located. They are opening a second tasting in downtown Napa at the corner of First and Main. **MAP 23**

**Viader** - Deer Park - Wines: Bordeaux style blends. Syrah, Tempranillo. 1120 Deer Park Road Deer Park CA 94574 www.viader.com (707) 963-3816 TF: $$$$ Hrs: 10-4:30 by Appt

This is a family-run winery that makes world class wines and sits on the slopes below Howell Mountain. The staff is good and they do a great tasting. The grape growing and winemaking has a European style, which is not surprising since the owner, Delia Viader, was born in Argentina and grew up in Europe. The views from the very modern tasting room are spectacular. They do modest tours and sit down tastings so plan at least 90 minutes for your visit. The entrance is half the way up the mountain, an easy drive from the valley floor, but the gate is on the left at a very sharp, climbing curve so be careful of the cars coming down the hill. **MAP 13**

**Vincent Arroyo Winery** - A Friendly Family-Run Winery  - Wines: Cab Sauv, Merlot, Petite Sirah, Chard, Sangiovese, Port, Blends.    2361 Greenwood Ave.  Calistoga  CA  94515.  www.vincentarroyo.com    (707) 942-6995  TF: $   Hrs: 10-4 Appt

They are located just north of downtown Calistoga. The tasting bar is in the barrel room, and the overall feeling is that of a small working winery without any pretensions.  The dogs are friendly, the wines are good and the grapes come from within walking distance. The Petite Sirah is very good and is practically their signature wine. They have some picnic tables and they are open by appointment simply because their production is low and the demand is high. Give them a call for a last minute appointment. They are located just south of Chateau Montelena.  **MAP 11**

**Vine Cliff Winery** - A Yountville Jewel   - Wines: Cab Sauv, Chard, Merlot. 7400 Silverado Trail  Yountville CA 94599   www.vinecliff.com  (707) 944-1364   TF: $$$$   Hrs: 10-5  by Appt

This is a jewel of a winery in its own canyon just off the Silverado Trail, north of the Yountville Cross Rd. They have beautiful gardens and gorgeous caves that are part of the tour. They do a very good tour that starts in the barrel/tasting room. They have a great staff and excellent wines. They are often open to last minute appointments, but their reputation is very good and so it is better to plan ahead. Their gate is normally closed so either call ahead or call from the gate and hope that they can see you. **MAP 18**

**Vineyard 29** - Appointment in Advance   - Wines: Cab Sauv, Cab Franc, Sauv Blanc, Zin, Blends.  2929 Highway 29 N.  St. Helena  CA  94574   www. vineyard29.com  (707) 963-9292  TF: $$$$$, Hrs: Tue-Sat by Appt

This is a remarkable property north of St. Helena with a state of the art winery, situated on prime bench land, with great views of the valley. It normally takes 2 to 4 weeks to set up an appointment and then plan on 1 ½ hrs for the tasting and tour. This is not a child or pet friendly winery. The wines are excellent, the technology is stunning, the people are interesting and it is a beautiful place. The name of course comes from the address. **MAP 10**

**Vineyard 7 & 8** - Spring Mountain WOW - Wines: Cab Sauv, Chard.  4028 Spring Mountain Road  St. Helena  CA  94574   www.vineyard7and8.com  (707) 963-9425  TF: $$$   Hrs: by Appt, closed weekends. This remarkable, winery sits close to the top of Spring Mountain. It is for the enthusiast and tastings are private. When you enter the property, it looks like a house, but when you see it from the back, you realize that this is a very serious winery. The name comes from the numerological significance of the numerology of those two numbers. It has great views of the valley and the winery is designed to enjoy them. Plan on 1 ½ hrs for the tasting and tour. **MAP 12**

**Vintner's Collective** Tasting Room - Downtown Tasting Room    1245 Main St. Napa CA 94559    www.vintnerscollective.com    (707) 255-7150    TF: $$$ - $$$$  Hrs: 11-6  **MAP 21**

**Von Strasser Winery** - Diamond Mountain Jewel  - Wines: Cab Sauv, Cab Franc, Zin, Blends.    1510 Diamond Mountain Rd. Calistoga CA 94515 www.vonstrasser.com    (707) 942-0930    TF: $$$ - $$$$    Hrs: 10:30-4:30 by Appt. The tasting room that most everyone sees is simple, small and friendly. They have a great staff and great wines. They are tucked up in the canyons of Diamond Mountain, next door to Reverie Winery. They also do a wonderful cave tours and tastings that including chocolate. They have lovely outdoor patio for events. They are easy to reach on Diamond Mountain Road. **MAP 10**

**Waterstone Winery** - Taste at Oxbow Tasting Room  - Wines: Chard, Rose', Pinot Gris, Merlot, Cab Sauv.   708 First Street  Napa  CA  94559 www.waterstonewines.com  (707) 265-9600  TF: $$,  Hrs: 11-6 or 7  The Oxbow tasting rooms are remarkable for their high quality and Waterstone is a perfect example of that. They make some very nice wines and the tasting room is elegant but comfortable. **MAP 21**

**White Cottage Ranch Winery** - Howell Mountain  - Wines: Merlot, Cab Sauv, Cab Franc, Sangiovese, Zin and Syrah.   555 College Rd Angwin  CA 94508  www.WhiteCottageRanch.com  (707) 965-0516  TF: PIE  Hrs: by Appt.  This winery may seem out of the way, up on the mountain, but it is worth the trip. They have a pretty, conference-style tasting room on a great property, all run by a family that has spent their life making wine, and it is clear in the flavors. **MAP 13**

**Whitehall Lane Winery** - Fun with Wonderful Wines  - Wines: Cab Sauv, Merlot, Chard, Belmuscato Dessert Wine.   1563 St Helena Hwy (Hwy 29). S. St. Helena CA 94574  www.whitehalllane.com    (707) 963-7035  TF: $$ Hrs: 11-5:45. This is a fun winery with a great staff and excellent wines. The very modern tasting room has a bit of a bar feel, but it allows diverse groups to mix. **MAP 18**

**William Harrison Vineyards** - A Great Story  - Wines: Cab Sauv, Cab Franc, Chard, Blends.   1443 Silverado Trail  St. Helena  CA 94574  www. whwines.com    (707) 963-8310   TF: $$     Hrs: 11-5 Thu-Mon

This is a slightly rustic and clearly eccentric tasting room for a winery family with a great story that goes back to the 1500's in Italy. The wines are very interesting and the location is great. Watch out for the bear, the stuffed bear that is! **Map 19**

**William Hill Estate** - Surprising Grandeur  - Wines: Chard, Merlot, Cab Sauv, Cab Franc, Malbec, Petit Verdot, Estate Meritage.   1761 Atlas Peak Rd. Napa CA 94558   www.williamhillestate.com  (707) 265-3024    TF: $$ - $$$$$   Hrs: 10-5  by Appt, instant,   Tours by prior appt

This is a great site, with a picnic area under an arbor. The building is very dramatic and it has had several big owners. Currently it is owned by the Gallo family who has started investing in the Napa Valley. The wines are serious and well-made. **Map 17**

**Yates Family Vineyard** - Mt Veeder - Wines: Cab Sauv, Cab Franc, Merlot - 3104 Redwood Rd Napa  www.YatesFamilyVineyard.com  (707) 226-1800 TF: PIE  Hrs: By Appt  **MAP 16**

**Zahtila Vineyards** - **Now Laura Michael** - Same Owners - Very Small - Wines: Cab Sauv, Zin, Chard.  2250 Lake County Hwy.  Calistoga  CA  94515 www.zahtilavineyards.com   (707) 942-9251  TF: $ (inc. logo glass)    Hrs: 10-5 by Appt

This is a charming, small winery just minutes from downtown Calistoga that makes nice wines and pours them with that friendly inclusiveness that makes Calistoga shine. Take the time to drop in and enjoy their wines.  **MAP 10**

**ZD Wines** - Silverado Savvy  - Wines: Chard, Pinot Noir, Cab Sauv, Blends. 8383 Silverado Trail  Napa  CA  94558   www.zdwines.com  (800) 487-7757 TF: $$ -$$$  Hrs: 10-4:30

They have a friendly, relaxed, but gorgeous tasting room, a nice staff, a small gift area and some very good wine. They often get passed by because they are below the road on a downhill section of the Silverado Trail, so you don't see them until you're at the driveway. They are down the hill, to the south of Mumm Napa on the Silverado Trail. This is a winery worth visiting, organic, with a great family history. As you leave the tasting room, notice the sign 'Organic since 1999'. **Map 19**

## For Updates and Additions Buy our Napa Valley Wine Tour App

## for iPhone and Droid

# About the Authors, Plus Other Books & Resources

**Ralph & Lahni de Amicis,** *Your Friends in Wine Country,* *guides, authors and TV Hosts* who tour with clients in Napa, Sonoma, San Francisco and beyond. This is their 8th book about wine touring. They also host the TV show Wine Country @ Work about the hospitality industry, and author two of the world's top selling Wine Tour Apps. They work in several languages, to a greater of lesser extent, including English, Spanish, Italian, French, German and Portuguese. Reach them regarding tours through their website **www.AmicisTours.com** or directly to **Lahni@AmicisTours.com**.

**The Amicis Winery Guides** is the book series that experienced travelers rely upon. Filled with good advice and great maps, they provide a local guide's insights about maximizing the tasting room experience while safely navigating these country roads. They include numerous mapped tours, a comprehensive winery directory, plus restaurant, hotels and B&B directories. These books will help you make the best use of your time, for a day trip or a week long adventure. They were created to help answer the five questions and more:

> **What to expect in the winery?**
> **What to wear?**
> **Do we have a good map?**
> **Do we have a route that won't waste our time?**
> **Where should we eat?**

## Amicis Winery Guide: Dream Tours of Napa & Sonoma

ISBN: 978-1-931163-22-4 Price: $21.95

Digital ISBN: 978-1-931163-27-9 $9.99

This is the wine tourist's most comprehensive guide for enjoying both Napa and Sonoma, with 70 maps, 31 planned theme tours, and a detailed directory of 450 wineries that happily welcome visitors. *Also Available Digitally*

**It includes:** How to create the best daytrip strategy, what to wear, how to stretch your tasting endurance and most enjoy the tasting room experience. Plus, the keys for finding the best picnic spots and restaurants, shopping, lodgings and scenic drives. How to economically ship wine, enjoyably travel with kids, joining wine clubs, when to hire a car and driver, and much more! Increasingly popular in each new edition, the Guide is a great tool for planning multiple trips to wine country.

## AWG: Napa Dream Tours, 3rd Edition

Book, 5.5 x 8.5, 224 pages ISBN#: 978-1-931163-21-9 $14.95

Digital ISBN: 978-1-931163-28-6 $8.99

For touring Napa this guide provides 44 Easy Driving Maps and 21 detailed, Connect-the-Dots Dream Tours. 250 Winery Directory. *Also Available Digitally.*

## AWG: Sonoma Dream Tours, 3rd Edition

Book, 5.5 x 8.5, 180 pages

ISBN#: 978-1-931163-20-0 $14.95

For touring Napa this guide provides 29 Easy Driving Maps and 10 detailed, Connect-the-Dots Dream Tours. 200 Winery Directory. *Also Available Digitally.*

## The Wine Diet, It's Not Just for Breakfast Anymore

Book, 5.5 x 8.5, 136 pages, Color Photos

ISBN#: 978-1-931163-23-1 $14.95, Digital $5.99 from Kindle

Wine tourism is the best kind of adult entertainment, a wonderfully social mix of education, scenery, flavors and inebriation. This helpful collection of insights about wine country comes from Ralph & Lahni de Amicis, coincidentally Wine Tour Guides and Naturopathic Physicians. When they suggest you drink two glasses of wine and call them in the morning, they know what they're talking about. This is what they share with clients to help them feel more comfortable in the tasting room and more knowledgeable at the dining table. They offer guidelines about the healthiest way to consume wine and insights about the joys of traveling among the vineyards. This insider's perspective of wine tasting and travel is paired with the authors' beautiful collection of photos of vineyards and wineries.

# The Ergo Dynamic Work Place Series

## Is it Time to Redesign the Oval Office?
## Thoughts on the Power of Positioning

This entertaining collection of short essays is aimed at changing your perspective about how you affect your work place and how it affects you. Today more people in the USA are programming applications than working on farms. The workplace today, from the Oval Office on out, is about managing information at desks. People are trained to work at desks from Elementary school through college. They are mostly told where to sit by architects, administrators, teachers and bosses. But, if you want to perform to your greatest potential you need to shake off the preconceptions from that experience and learn the language of work place design. Kindle Version, ISBN 978-1-931163-45-3, $3.99.

## The Dream Desk Questionnaire
*Improving Personal & Team Performance*
*Through Recognizing Your ErgoDynamic Personality*

*Tell us what you want to improve and we'll tell you who and what to move!* Most people spend their entire careers being told where to sit, working in spaces that limit their genius, their performance and their job satisfaction. The Dream Desk Questionnaire, with its 7 Multiple Choice Questions & 43 Personalized Answers identifies your ErgoDynamic Preferences. It shows how using the Power of Positioning to choose and create Work Spaces will unleash your talents, promote ethical leadership skills and tremendous team cooperation. This is the secret weapon of many truly successful people, and you can use these seven techniques to attain greater success in your own career now, and in the future.
Illustrated, Print Version, 92 pages, 6 x 9 in. ISBN 978-1-931163-37-8, $9.95.
Digital Version: ISBN 978-1-931163-38-5, $5.95

## The Student's Dream Desk Questionnaire
After a lifetime of being told where to go, where to sit & where to work, the Dream Desk Questionnaire, with its 7 multiple choice questions & 43 personalized answers helps identify your individual, Ergonomic talents.
Illustrated, Print Version, 92 pages, 6 x 9 in. ISBN 978-1-931163-35-4, $9.95.
Digital Version: ISBN 978-1-931163-36-1, $5.95

# Find Out More About Wine Country by Watching Episodes of

## Wine Country @ Work
*from Napa Valley TV*

This monthly show offers an inside look at the hospitality and wine community that makes the world's most popular Wine Tour Destination work. It explores how a work force of 10,000 people deal with three million visitors yearly, most of whom are loopy. Produced and Hosted by Authors and Tour Guides Ralph & Lahni de Amicis, and filmed on site at wineries and other local venues, it provides a fascinating story about the people who havecome from all over the world to work in this beautiful place and in this unique industry.

## www.AmicisTours.com
## www.SpaceAndTime.com